D1350799

Springwood Junction

Then: 24 May 1959
Situated in a deep cutting between Huddersfield Tunnel and Gledholt Tunnel, Springwood Junction signalbox must have been a dismal place to work. This was the location of the junction where the ex-L&YR line to Penistone diverged from the ex-LNWR line to Standedge. Here Patricroft-based 'Jubilee' No 45558 *Manitoba* is seen passing on its departure from Huddersfield with a Leeds-Manchester stopping service.

Now: 1 November 1994
Today the track has been rationalised. The down main line passes through the left hand tunnel — although not visible through the undergrowth — whilst up trains use the track on which Class 158 No 158811, forming the 13.25 York-Manchester train, is utilising. Services to Penistone and Sheffield use the track on the far right.
Author (2)

Brighouse Marshalling Yards

Then: 17 July 1960
Brighouse used to be a hive of activity with the four main lines and extensive marshalling yards; however, by 1960 the yards were getting quite empty. The station was out of sight to the left of the 'S' bend in the track. In the later 1950s and early 1960s the loaded and empty coal trains produced a virtually continuous procession of 'WD' 2-8-0s, as shown by this photograph of No 90016 heading east.

Now: 30 May 1993
After the closure of the yard, two through running lines were taken out of use and were used to store surplus wagons. Over the years the site has been cleared and now the two running lines run through without a single cross-over and the surplus land sold for industrial development. A couple of Class 31s, Nos 31205 and 31276, are shown working wrong line one Sunday on a permanent way maintenance train. The line has been freight only for many years, although it is used reasonably frequently for diversions when the Standedge route is closed for maintenance. There are proposals that could lead to passenger services over the line being restored, but there is no timetable at this stage for their reintroduction.
Author (2)

LONDON MIDLAND
THEN & NOW

GAVIN MORRISON

IAN ALLAN
Publishing

Contents

First published 1995

ISBN 978-0-7110-2371-0

All rights reserved. No part of this book may be reproduced or transmitted in any form or by any means, electronic or mechanical, including photocopying, recording or by any information storage and retrieval system, without permission from the Publisher in writing.

© Ian Allan Ltd 1995

Designed by Alan C. Butcher

Published by Ian Allan Publishing

an imprint of Ian Allan Ltd, Terminal House, Station Approach, Shepperton, Surrey TW17 8AS.
This edition produced by TAJ Books - 2007
Printed in China

Introduction

This is the second in Ian Allan's series of 'Then & Now' volumes covering the English parts of the London Midland & Scottish, the biggest of the 'Big Four'. It covers Carlisle to Holyhead to Bristol to Shoeburyness, and most points in between. This, of course, created some problems in trying to cover such a wide area within the winter months of December, January and February, but the time scale was outside my control. The 'Then' locations were primarily selected from the contents of the Ian Allan Library and from my own collection. With a limit of around 300 locations, it is obvious that in one volume one can only give a limited coverage, and it will be easy to find locations which are omitted. I hope that the selection will give an overall picture of the changes that have taken place.

It has been a very interesting exercise, as I have visited places, some of them local, which I have not been to for over 35 years. In fact, one location on the outskirts of Bradford had changed so much that I couldn't find the spot where I had taken a picture in 1966. I suspect that I would have had to get permission to stand in the middle of a factory floor from an engineering company.

I have been very surprised how easy it has been to find local people who could tell me exactly where to stand to take the appropriate picture, although one had to be careful to select those in the 50-plus age bracket.

The fate of many disused railway sites has been varied; most have been used for housing or small industrial complexes, but other uses I came across were fire stations, leisure centres and, of course, supermarkets. I have visited enough supermarket car parks in the last three months to last me well into 1996. On a more positive note, some old stations have been developed into superb houses, and to the owners of these properties who allowed me to photograph them I am very grateful, especially to the gentleman who was very worried that my presence would upset his dogs which won many prizes at international shows. My visits did have the occasional benefit to the house owners; I was able to explain to a lady in Grassington why there were so many stones a few inches below the surface of her garden, as it was on top of the trackbed.

To those readers who may have a collection of railway photographs taken around 30 years ago, or even a much shorter time, I would recommend that they occasionally take a selection of 'Then' pictures out and revisit the sites today; I am sure they would find it a very interesting experience.

One aspect of the project has been the difficulty I have had in trying to get some variety into the motive power in the pictures.

I am afraid the Class 158 Sprinters seem to turn up everywhere. Occasionally, it has not been possible to stand in exactly the same position; this is particularly the case on the electrified lines where road and footbridges have vanished. In these cases the viewpoint has been modified accordingly with an explanation in the caption.

You will no doubt form your own conclusions as to where you think the changes have been most dramatic, but Manchester Victoria and Normanton must be near the top of the list. Whilst many stations have altered little, it is generally the immediate surrounding area which has seen the most dramatic changes. I suppose one has to admit that a book such as this gives a rather depressing picture from a railway enthusiast's point of view, and I doubt if it will get any better in the immediate future so, in my case, I should be grateful for having been around when much of what is shown here was fully in use.

To produce a book within the timescale has needed considerable planning, as the weather has not exactly helped — I nearly got trapped by snow in Dentdale on the Settle-Carlisle line, in my case a repeat performance of an event in 1963. I have personally covered 6,700 miles in obtaining the photographs, not to mention the distance covered by my friends Brian Morrison, who sorted out the area around London where I would have got very lost, and John Turner, who was doing a splendid job for me south of Birmingham until he unfortunately broke his leg on an embankment in Gloucestershire. This upset the schedule and caused one or two omissions, especially in South Wales. I am glad to say he is now out and about with the camera again, and to both of them I extend my thanks.

I must also thank those at Ian Allan who have assisted me in many ways to meet the deadline. A special word of thanks must go to my friend Keith Marshall, whose expert guidance with the Ordnance Survey maps has allowed me to get around much more quickly than would otherwise have been possible; I suspect without his aid I would still be looking for Distington Junction in Cumbria.

Looking back on the areas which I have visited, the one which I regret not having photographed more in the past would be Cumbria, especially places such as Workington, Maryport, Moor Row, etc — the photographic opportunities must have been fantastic, and one sees so few pictures in the railway press.

I hope that you enjoy browsing through the book, and that some of the pictures will bring back happy memories.

Gavin Morrison
Mirfield
March 1995

Bibliography

LMS Engine Sheds Volume 2, Chris Hawkins and George Reeve, Wild Swan
Clinker's Register of Closed Passenger Stations 1830-1980, C. R. Clinker, Avon Anglia
A-Z of Rail Reopenings, Railways Development Society
The North Wales Coast Railway, P. E. Baughan, Martin Bairstow
The 'Little' North Western Railway, D. Binns, Wyvern Publications
The Manchester & Leeds Railway, M. Bairstow, Martin Bairstow
The Leeds Huddersfield & Manchester Railway, M. Bairstow, Martin Bairstow
Railways Around East Lancashire, C. R. Wilby, Wyvern Publications
Railways Around Skipton, D. Binns, Wyvern Publications
The Leeds, Settle-Carlisle Railway, M. Bairstow, Martin Bairstow
Portrait of the Settle-Carlisle, David Joy, Dalesman

St Albans Abbey

Then: 14 January 1978
The LNWR branch from Watford opened on 5 May 1858. The station, became known as 'St Albans Abbey' in the 1920s. The ex-LNWR station was also the terminus of a Great Northern branch from Hatfield from the 1860s until its closure to passenger services in 1951. By the date of this photograph facilities at St Albans had already been reduced, as a two-car Cravens DMU arrives to form the 11.03 working to Watford. The train is formed of DMBS No 50381 leading DTSL No 56148.
Now: 12 February 1995
Little has changed at this austere terminus other than the construction of the office block and the electrification of the line. On this particular day the shuttle to Watford Junction was in the hands of Class 313 EMU No 313003
Brian Morrison (2)

The epitome of LMS main line steam at its zenith — the 'Coronation Scot' climbs Camden Bank behind streamlined Stanier 'Coronation' Pacific No 6221 *Queen Elizabeth* on 23 September 1938. In the foreground 'Jubilee' class 4-6-0 No 5563 *Australia* backs up the hill to Camden shed. *E. R. Wethersett*

London & North Western Railway

At one time the largest joint stock company in the world, the London & North Western Railway could proudly claim to be the 'Premier Line'. Formed on 16 July 1846, the company's origins lay with many of the earliest main line railways in the country — the Liverpool & Manchester (opened in 1830 and already absorbed into the Grand Junction), the Grand Junction (the first true main line, which linked Birmingham with Warrington and which opened on 4 July 1837), the Manchester & Birmingham (which linked Crewe with Manchester) and the London & Birmingham (which opened between London and Birmingham in stages between 1837 and 1838). Another part, albeit jointly controlled with the L&YR, was the North Union (which represented a combination of the Preston & Wigan Railway — opened in 1838 — and the Wigan Branch Railway of 1832) which made Preston the northern terminus of the West Coast route until the completion of the Preston & Lancaster Junction Railway in June 1840 — a railway whose early history was controversial.

Even before the 1846 amalgamation, the constituent companies had already embarked on a process of expansion and acquisition that was ultimately to see the LNWR stretch from London to Carlisle and from South Wales to East Anglia. The Grand Junction, for example, had acquired lines such as the Warrington & Newton and the Chester & Crewe — the latter forming an essential part in the future main line along the North Wales coast to Holyhead and helping to make Crewe — a name redolent with LNWR history — into a major junction. The London & Birmingham had also extended its operation to include a branch via Northampton to Peterborough, which opened in 1845.

Even before the amalgamation was 12 months old, the LNWR had continued to expand. The Lancaster & Carlisle Railway was opened to Oxenholme on 22 September 1846 and thence to Carlisle on 17 December 1846. The Trent Valley line, from Rugby to Stafford, opened to passenger services on 1 December 1847. The Lancaster & Carlisle Railway along with the Lancaster & Preston (with which it was amalgamated in the 1850s) were both formerly incorporated into the LNWR in 1879.

Another company ultimately to pass into the control of the LNWR was the Chester & Holyhead Railway, which was authorised to construct a line linking the Chester & Crewe with the port of Holyhead. The first section of the line, from Chester to Bangor, opened on 1 May 1848, whilst the remainder, including the dramatic Britannia Bridge over the Menai Strait,

followed on 18 March 1850. The Chester & Holyhead company passed into LNWR ownership in 1858.

The LNWR continued to expand through the mid to late 19th century through both the acquisition of existing railways, as well as through the construction of new lines. Amongst those railways taken over were the Leeds, Dewsbury & Manchester (in 1847), the Bedford & Cambridge (1865), the Merthyr, Tredegar & Abergavenny (1866), the Cockermouth & Workington/Whitehaven Junction (1866), the Cromford & High Peak (1867), the Central Wales (1868) and the Denbigh, Ruthin & Corwen (in 1879). Amongst lines built was the Winwick Junction-Golborne Junction section of the West Coast main line that was opened on 1 August 1864.

In addition to the North Union, the LNWR was also jointly involved with a number of joint railways, these included the Great Western Railway in the Shrewsbury & Hereford, the Furness in the Whitehaven, Cleator & Egremont and the Midland, Caledonian and Glasgow & South Western in the Portpatrick & Wigtownshire Joint.

By the turn of the century there were few parts of England and Wales that were not influenced to some extent by the LNWR. It could justifiably look back on more than half a century of development, but that situation was to change all too rapidly. Although in 1922 it absorbed the Lancashire & Yorkshire Railway, thus extending its control in the north considerably, the LNWR was to lose its independence at the Grouping when, horror of horrors, it was linked with its long term competitor the Midland Railway.

In the 70 years since the Grouping, much has occurred to alter the nature of the LNWR inheritance. There have been the inevitable line closures — those that have succumbed include many of the most romantic lines such as those linking Oxford and Cambridge, Penrith and Cockermouth, and Abergavenny and Merthyr, as well as many of the lines in rural Buckinghamshire and Northamptonshire. But the main lines in general survive and, with electrification of the West Coast route and its branches to Liverpool and Manchester, would seem to have an assured future despite the current uncertainties. Crewe remains an important junction and ex-LNWR lines still run along the North Wales coast to Holyhead, down the branch to Blaenua Ffestiniog, along the Cumbrian coast between Whitehaven and Maryport, and between Manchester and Leeds. Although modernised, there remains much to remind the well-informed traveller of the LNWR inheritance.

Euston station — The Doric Arch

Then: 3 June 1953
There can be no more fitting opening to the section on the London & North Western Railways than Philip Hardwick's superb Doric Arch at London Euston station. Built in 1838, the famous entrance to the LNWR's station was floodlight in 1953 to mark the Coronation of HM Queen Elizabeth II.

Now: December 1994
Few could have imagined in 1953 that within a decade the Doric Arch would cease to exist but that was to prove the case, as it, and the rest of the old Euston station, were swept away as modernisation took hold. Whilst the new station may be functional, one has to admit that it does not have quite the appeal of its Victorian counterpart. It is interesting to note that, more than three decades after the demolition of the Arch, the loss is now widely regarded as having stimulated the growth of conservation of Victorian structures and that research as to the ultimate fate of the building continues. Who knows, but the 21st century may yet dawn with the reconstruction of this epitome of the railway age.
Ian Allan Library/Brian Morrison

Euston station — Buffer stops

Then: 1 September 1952
Warrington (Dallam)-allocated 'Jubilee' No 45655 *Keith* simmers gently at the buffer stops at Platform No 2 having brought the up 'Welshman' express in.
Now: 30 December 1994
Today the cast-iron of the Victorian station is long gone, swept away in the modernisation of the station from 1962 onwards, and the building has about as much atmosphere as a hospital operating theatre. Two West Coast main line DVTs, Nos 82106 and 82103, stand silently in platforms Nos 1 and 2 ready for another trip northwards.
Brian Stephenson/Brian Morrison

Euston station — Country end

Then: 28 August 1952
The London Midland Region official photographer was present to record the first occasion the rebuilt 'Princess Royal', No 46202 *Princess Anne*, hauled the 8.30am express to Liverpool. Looking immaculate in its green livery against the drab Euston surroundings, the locomotive awaits the green flag to depart.

Now: 30 December 1994
Forty-two years later it is difficult to imagine that Euston used to have platform surfaces of wood, although in wet conditions the modern tiling seems to require sawdust to reduce its slipperiness. Here we see Class 87/0 No 87004 *Britannia* waiting to depart on the 11.40 service to Preston.
Ian Allan Library/Brian Morrison

Camden Bank

Then: 23 September 1938
I suppose this picture captures the really glorious years of the railways in Britain. What a sight and sound 'Princess Coronation' No 6221 *Queen Elizabeth* must have made in its blue livery; equally the clean 'Jubilee' No 5563 *Australia* must have been striking in maroon.

Primrose Hill Tunnel

Then: 21 July 1951
The down 'Mancunian' hauled by a very dirty rebuilt 'Royal Scot' No 46116 *Irish Guardsman* heads northwards towards Primrose Hill Tunnel, the first tunnel on the West Coast main line out of Euston, with Caprotti-fitted Class 5 No 44749, of Longsight, light engine on the left.

High Road

Then: 22 July 1931
One of the 47 Bowen-Cooke LNWR 4-6-2Ts which were built between 1910 and 1916, No 6974, hustles a down commuter train northwards. The locomotives were withdrawn between 1936 and 1941.

Now: 18 February 1995
Class 87/0 No 87032 *Kenilworth* is a poor substitute for the great days of steam as it climbs effortlessly out of Euston on the 12.30 service to Glasgow. The bridge, retaining wall and a number of background buildings remain, but 'Upside Carriage Shed' is no more and the background is dominated by high-rise flats.
E. R. Wethersett (Ian Allan Library)/Ken Brunt

Now: 18 February 1995
Today the up and down main lines are still in position, whilst the retaining wall and a number of buildings in the background are also still extant. However, the track layout has been considerably altered, with the provision of an underpass for the slow lines. Class 86/2 No 86256 *Pebble Mill* is caught hauling the 13.35 Euston-Wolverhampton service.
E. R. Wethersett (Ian Allan Library)/Brian Morrison

Now: 21 January 1995
Only the suburban platforms now remain, although the background terrace has changed remarkably little albeit now dominated by a new office block. The 10.54 Euston-Birmingham (New Street) service, formed of Class 321/4s Nos 321431 and 321417, rushes past the site of the now-demolished platforms.
E. R. Wethersett (Ian Allan Library)/Brian Morrison

Willesden West London Branch Junction

Then: 10 April 1939
A superb picture of Midland Compound No 1160 piloting unrebuilt 'Royal Scot' No 6101 *Royal Scots Grey* on an unidentified down train on Easter Monday 1939. Note the signalbox and the fine signals in the background.

Kensington (Addison Road/Olympia)

Then: 23 May 1949
The West London Joint and the West London Extension provided a link between the LNWR at Willesden and the lines south of the Thames at Clapham Junction. The first section from Willesden to Kensington opened in 1844, but the extension to Clapham was not opened until 1863. The most important intermediate station was that at Kensington, which was rebuilt in the 1860s. The West London was jointly controlled by the GWR and LNWR; the extension line also involved the LSWR and LBSCR. This interesting picture shows Willesden-allocated '4F' No 44442 heading a northbound freight, whilst in the background postwar development was in full swing.

Willesden Junction

Then: 21 September 1935
This fine study sees Compound No 1150, then allocated to Camden, pausing at Willesden Junction with an up slow train. Note the somewhat derelict appearance of the wood panelling on the high level platforms.

Now: 21 January 1995
Both the signalbox and the signals have now vanished, and the photographic location has as a consequence lost some of its appeal. Class 90 No 90005 *Financial Times* heads north with the 11.50 Euston-Manchester (Piccadilly) service.
E. R. Wethersett (Ian Allan Library)/Brian Morrison

Now: 31 May 1994
Today the route still provides a very wide variety of traffic and motive power. Illustrated is a Class 117 DMU No L701 (formed of DMBS No 51350 and DMS No 51392) entering Olympia on the 13.03 North London Railway's service from Clapham Junction to Willesden Junction. Class 60 No 60043 *Yes Tor* heads in the opposite direction at the head of a rake of Yeoman hoppers. The signalbox has vanished, a victim of the electrification of the route and the resignalling associated with the use of the line for Eurostar trains to North Pole depot.
C. C. B. Herbert/Brian Morrison

Now: 21 January 1995
The track on which the Compound was standing, on the right of the picture, is now rusting over and seemingly little used. Trains ceased to stop at the platforms illustrated in the 'Then' photograph in September 1962. The tracks were realigned and the platforms demolished as part of the 25kV electrification scheme. Class 321/4 No 321407 passes with the 10.31 Milton Keynes Central-Euston service. Note the staircase still links the high level station with the ground.
E. R. Wethersett (Ian Allan Library)/Brian Morrison

Kensal Rise

Then: September 1951
This station was the first on the line east from Willesden Junction towards Hampstead and Gospel Oak.
Now: 21 January 1995
The station buildings have all been demolished and little remains save the platforms and the background housing. Services on the North London line from Richmond to Stratford still call at the station and Class 313 No 313021 is pictured working the 09.30 Stratford (Low Level)-Richmond service.
Ian Allan Library/Brian Morrison

South Kenton

Then: 28 August 1954
The up 'Royal Scot' pictured in the days when 13-coach and longer trains were normal. 'Princess Coronation' No 46230 *Duchess of Buccleuch*, which would have worked through from Glasgow being a Polmadie-based locomotive, nears the end of its journey. The fireman is leaning out, looking relaxed as the hard work would now be over.
Now: 21 April 1990
The lineside trees now hide the buildings in the background as a Mark 3 DVT heads the 13.55 Woverhampton-Euston service. Class 86/2 No 86260 *Bishop Eric Treacy* provides the power at the rear of the train. The bridge in the background of the 'Then' photograph was removed in the early 1960s with the electrification of the route.
E. R. Wethersett (Ian Allan Library)/Brian Morrison

Kenton

The: 11 October 1930

Two of the famous Bowen-Cooke 'Prince of Wales' class 4-6-0s Nos 5684 *Arabic* and 5685 *Persia* head a heavy Euston-Cardington funeral special which was run in connection with the R101 airship disaster. There were 246 of the class built and all were withdrawn between 1933 and 1949.

Now: 21 April 1990

Little has changed over the intervening 60 years except for the appearance of the electrification masts and catenary. This location now represents one of the few locations on the line where it is still possible to obtain a reasonable picture from an overbridge. Class 87/0 No 87024 *Lord of the Isles* rushes past with the 16.30 Euston-Blackpool North train; this through service has now been discontinued and passengers for Blackpool must change at Preston.

E. R. Wethersett (Ian Allan Library)/Brian Morrison

Carpender's Park Station

Then: 30 July 1952

Carpender's Park station opened in 1914, primarily to serve the local golf course, at which time the wooden platforms and buildings were provided. With the growth of commuting, the number of passengers increased dramatically and this growth continued with the construction of housing estates in the area.

Now: 19 November 1990

Apart from the presence of the railway track, virtually the only common feature between these two photographs is the presence of the pylon on the right-hand skyline. The station itself was completely rebuilt in 1957. The track alignment has been eased, the overbridge has disappeared and the station now serves only the suburban lines. Class 90 No 90019 *Penny Black*, then in InterCity livery and today in Res, passes the station at speed on the down 13.00 Euston-Manchester (Piccadilly) express.

Ian Allan Library/Brian Morrison

Stanmore

Then: July 1952
The short branch from Harrow
& Wealdstone on the West
Coast main line and the
Middlesex village of Stanmore
opened on 18 December 1890.
Ivatt 2-6-2T No 41220 is
pictured working the branch
passenger train at the terminus
some two months before the
branch lost its passenger
services.
Now: February 1995
The ex-LNWR branch
suffered in competition from
the more conveniently located
station that served the
Metropolitan Railway and, as
a result, passenger services

were withdrawn on
15 September 1952. Freight
services remained until final
closure on 5 October 1964.
The station site is now a
housing estate and a road has
been built on the old trackbed.
The former station house is
now a private residence, but its
former role is commemorated
by a plaque adjacent to an ivy-
clad doorway.
*Ian Allan Library/Brian
Morrison (2)*

Bushey Troughs

Then: 25 March 1953
This was a classic West Coast main line photographic location from as long ago as the LNWR era. 'Jubilee' No 45737 *Atlas* picks up water as it heads the up 9.45am 'Midlander' from Woverhampton. This train travelled via Birmingham, Coventry and Northampton, with a scheduled arrival time in Euston of 12.45pm.
Now: 11 April 1992
Today it is still possible to photograph the trains even with electrification, although the troughs are now but a distant memory. Mark 3 DVT No 82147 heads the 12.30 InterCity service from Manchester (Piccadilly) towards Euston with Class 87/0 No 87028 *Lord President* providing the power from the rear of the train.
Brian Morrison (2)

Watford Junction

Then: 9 August 1952
In the age before electrification, Watford Junction represented a fine photographic location, as shown in this picture of Caprotti-fitted Class 5 No 44751 piloting 'Jubilee' No 45674 *Duncan* on a down Euston-Manchester express.
Now: 11 April 1992
Today one track has been removed, together with the platform canopy and Watford No 1 signalbox. Class 90 No 90007 *Lord Stamp* approaches the station with the 12.30 service from Euston to Birmingham (New Street).
Brian Morrison (2)

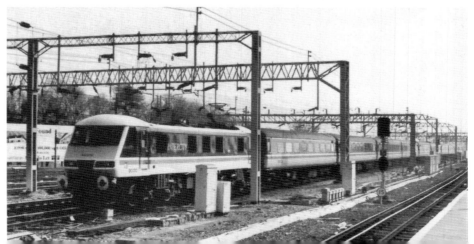

Watford Junction (St Albans Branch)

Then: 9 August 1952
The LNWR branch from Watford Junction to St Albans opened on 5 May 1858. It was originally proposed that the line would be extended through to Luton and Dunstable, but this line was never built. From 1952 the London Midland Region operated three sets of privately-sponsored three-car, four-wheeled DMU built by ACV (Sales) Ltd. One of the trio, painted in the two-tone grey with red lining livery, is seen arriving at Watford Junction with the 5.53pm service from St Albans Abbey.

Now: 12 February 1995
An interesting comparison of multiple-units sees Class 313 No 313003 operating on the 10.03 service from St Albans. Most of the immediate area around the station is now either offices or car parks.

Brian Morrison (2)

Watford Tunnel

Then: 9 August 1952

The summer picture of the 12 noon Wolverhampton/Birmingham-Euston express headed by 'Jubilee' No 45734 *Meteor* gives the impression that there were even more trees about in 1952 than today. The tunnel at Watford dates back to the construction of the London & Birmingham Railway in the 1830s and it was the only major structure completed by the original contractor without the necessity for the railway to be involved. Notice the triangular pediment over the tunnel's portal. When the West Coast main line was quadrupled at this point a second tunnel was built in the 1870s.

Now: 13 April 1994

A Northampton-Euston semi-fast train passes the same location formed of Class 321/4 EMU No 321404. Note how the lineside growth has been cut back, but is already reclaiming its earlier dominance.
Brian Morrison (2)

Cheddington

Then: Undated

Taken in pre-Grouping days, this shot of Cheddington sees an up train heading towards Euston over the London & North Western main line. The London & Birmingham Railway, predecessor of the LNWR, opened through from Rugby to London in April 1838.

Now: 17 February 1995

The general layout of the station remains unchanged although everything has been rebuilt. An unidentified up express headed by DVT No 82132 rushes past at about 100mph.
Ian Allan Library/Author

Leighton Buzzard

Then: July 1960
'Princess Coronation' No 46243 *City of Lancaster*, in terrible external condition, heads an assortment of coaches on a down express through the station. This scene was soon to change dramatically with the commencement of electrification work on the West Coast main line. The railway though Leighton Buzzard opened in April 1838.
Now: 17 February 1995
Electrification has arrived and the station has been modernised, and the trees have grown to block out the view of the houses in the background. A down express, headed by Class 86/2 No 86242 *James Kennedy GC*, rushes past on the fast line *en route* for Birmingham.
J. C. Baker/Author

Bletchley

Then: 28 March 1959
Bletchley is 46 miles from Euston and in the days of steam represented effectively the outer limits of the commuter services from Euston. The section through Bletchley, like all the London-Rugby route, opened in 1838. The importance of Bletchley to the LNWR grew with the opening of the lines to Oxford and Bedford on 20 May 1851 and 17 November 1846 respectively. Local BR Standard Class 4MT No 75038 is pictured leaving for Oxford, whilst Stanier Class 5 No 45146 heads towards Euston on a stopping train.

Now: 17 February 1995
Today's commuters are willing to travel much further, a result of the much improved timings that electrification has brought. It was, unfortunately, impossible to achieve the same elevation as the photographer in 1950, but it is still possible to see the many changes that have occurred over the past 35 years. On the right can be seen the Bletchley flyover, which was completed in 1962; today, the flyover is something of a white elephant as the line from Bletchley towards Oxford has been mothballed. Passenger services between Oxford and Bletchley were withdrawn on 1 January 1968 (although they have subsequently been reinstated between Oxford and Bicester). Passenger services continue to operate, however, to Bedford. Heading an up express towards Euston, DVT No 82121 rushes non-stop through the station.
S. Creer/Author

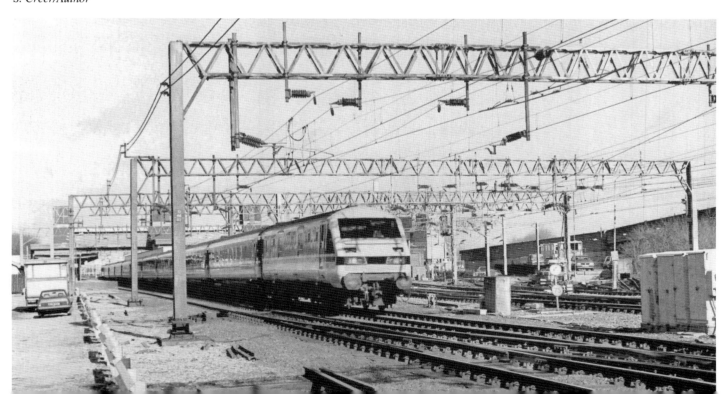

Great Linford

Then: 26 October 1963
The short branch from Wolverton to Newport Pagnell opened on 2 September 1867. There were two intermediate stations, Bradwell and Great Linford, and at the latter an Ivatt 2-6-2T is shown calling with the 1.30pm push-pull service from Newport Pagnell.
Now: 17 February 1995
The branch lost its passenger services on 7 September 1964 and freight ceased to operate over the line on 22 May 1967. The line has subsequently been dismantled, but this station has been transformed into a very pleasant footpath.
M. Mensing/Author

Northampton (Castle)

Then: May 1960
The LNWR reached Northampton with the completion of a branch from Blisworth which was opened on 13 May 1845. This was extended to Peterborough later the same year. The line through Northampton (Castle) was opened from the existing line at Northampton opened on 16 February 1859. The section from Rugby to Northampton opened on 1 December 1881, following the rebuilding of Castle station (and the demolition of the castle ruins from which it gained its name), and the line from Roade to Northampton followed on 3 April 1882. Class 4F No 44242 is pictured arriving at the station with a local freight from Blisworth.
Now: 17 February 1995
The station has been completely rebuilt and services over the Northampton loop are now electrified. The links to both Peterborough and Blisworth have both gone, although the stubs of both lines remain. Unfortunately, on the day the 'Now' photograph was taken, the overhead catenary had been blown down and so a decision was made not to wait for a train. Until the mid-1960s Northampton was also served by a branch off the ex-Midland main line from Bedford.
J. C. Baker/Author

Weedon

Then: 14 April 1962
This station was near the junction where the line to Warwick left the West Coast main line. A Stephenson Locomotive Society special, headed by the last active Midland Class 2P 4-4-0 No 40646, called here on its way back to Birmingham, although the station had been closed to passengers services since 15 September 1958.
Now: 31 December 1994
The station has been demolished and the line electrified. There is little evidence to indicate that there was ever a station at this point.
Author/J. Turner

Rugby

Then: 16 June 1951

Courtesy of the London & Birmingham Railway, the railways reached Rugby in 1838 and from that point the town became an important railway junction. LNWR lines radiated towards Birmingham, Northampton, Stafford, Leamington Spa, Market Harborough and Watford, whilst the Midland also served the town with its route north to Leicester. A later interloper saw the Great Central's London Extension pass over the LNWR lines at the south end of the station. Here the 2.30pm Euston-Liverpool express leaves past No 4 signalbox with more than adequate motive power in the form of 'Jubilee' No 45741 *Leinster* and rebuilt 'Royal Scot' No 46138 *The London Irish Regiment*.

Now: 30 December 1994

Although the Midland line to Leicester and the ex-LNWR lines to Market Harborough and Leamington Spa are now but a memory (except for a spur on the last-named serving a cement works), Rugby remains an important junction. Despite its importance, modernisation seems to have largely passed the station by, and the structure remains much as it was when rebuilt in the 1880s. Electrification has, however, brought modern motive power in the form of an immaculate Class 87/0 No 87025 *County of Cheshire* which is seen preparing to leave on the 13.00 Euston-Liverpool service.

A. F. Taylor/J. Turner

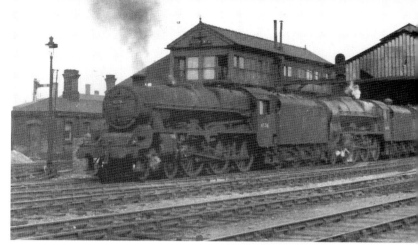

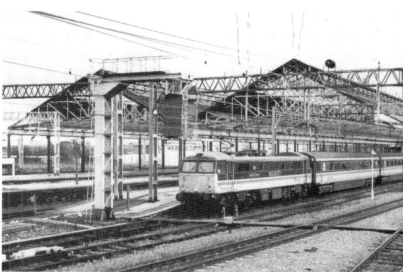

Southam & Long Itchington

Then: May 1958

This station was situated on the line between Weedon and Warwick. The route opened between Weedon and Daventry on 1 March 1888 and thence to Marton Junction on 1 August 1895. An Ivatt 2-6-2T is seen at the station with a push-pull working shortly before the withdrawal of passenger services.

Now: 30 December 1994

Passenger services between Leamington and Weedon over this line ceased on 15 September 1958 and the section between Southam and Napton closed completely in January 1963. The line remained open to serve a cement works at Southam, reached by the remains of the Rugby-Leamington branch, until final closure in the late 1980s. At the site of the station the trackbed and bridge survive, but all traces of the buildings have gone.

Ian Allan Library/J. Turner

Marton

Then: May 1958
Marton was the point where the Rugby-Leamington line met the route from Weedon. The line from Rugby to Leamington opened on 1 March 1851 and the line from Daventry to Marton Junction followed on 1 August 1895.

Now: 30 December 1994
Although passenger services to Weedon were withdrawn in 1958, those between Leamington and Rugby were to survive until 15 June 1959. The section of line between Leamington and Marton closed completely in 1966, but the section from Marton to Rugby remained open to give access to the now-closed line to the cement works at Southam. Although the trackbed and bridge still stand, there are no traces of the once fine station.
Ian Allan Library/J. Turner

Banbury (Merton Street)

Then: May 1951
This terminus was at the end of the LNWR branch from Bletchley which divided at Verney Junction from the line to Oxford. It opened on 1 May 1850. Stanier 2-6-4T No 42667 is shown waiting to leave with a service for Bletchley from the attractive station.

Now: 30 December 1994
Despite being one of the earliest recipients of new traction , in the form of lightweight single diesel units in the 1950s, the branch from Verney Junction closed to passenger services beyond Buckingham on 2 January 1961. Freight continued over the line until 2 December 1963, although final closure at Merton Street did not come until June 1966. As can be seen in this shot, all traces of the station seem to have vanished.
Ian Allan Library/J. Turner

Shilton

Then: August 1953
Blackpool-allocated 'Jubilee' No 45584 *North West Frontier* heads an up express through the station, which was situated south of Nuneaton on the West Coast main line.

Now: 4 February 1995
The station closed on 16 September 1957, although freight facilities were retained until 1965. All signs of the station have now gone and just the three through lines, now electrified, remain. With Class 87 No 87024 *Lord of the Isles* providing the power, the 06.10 Glasgow-Euston service rushes by at the 110mph line speed headed by DVT No 82142.
J. P. Delaney/Author

Nuneaton (south)

Then: March 1959
The Trent Valley line, from Stafford to Rugby, was opened in 1847 and provided an alternative to the existing main line through Birmingham. The first Nuneaton station dated from the line's opening, but it was rebuilt in 1909. Stanier '8F' No 48111 heads south with a loaded mineral train, whilst 'Jubilee' No 45731 *Perseverance* waits for the signals to clear with another up freight.

Now: 4 February 1995
Although the 1909 station remains largely intact, there are a number of detail differences — note, for example, the loss of the clock face from the tower. The trackwork has, however, been rationalised and the overhead for the 25kV has ruined an otherwise fine photographic location.
Class 158 No 158785 leaves on the 09.42 Birmingham-Cambridge train, whilst Transrail Class 56 No 56025 is stabled at the head of an up oil train.
H. H. Bleads/Author

Ashby Junction (Nuneaton)

Then: 18 April 1960
Situated just to the north of Nuneaton station, this was the junction between the Trent Valley main line and the joint LNWR/MR line from Coalville. One of the handsome unrebuilt 'Patriots', No 45546 *Fleetwood*, heads south on an Easter Monday special from Manchester to Euston with at least 12 coaches.

Now: 4 February 1995
The former high vantage point was no longer available, so this shot gives a slightly different angle. The link to Weddington Junction was severed on 17 August 1969. The ex-LNWR/MR joint line is also closed, although the section between Shackerstone and Shenton forms the preserved Battlefield line. With Class 90 No 90008 *The Birmingham Royal Mail* providing power from the rear, DVT No 82109 heads an up express past the site of the junction.
G. D. King/Author

Coventry

Then: May 1958
Bushbury-based 'Jubilee' No 45741 *Leinster* calls at the station with a down Euston-Wolverhampton express. The first station at Coventry dated from the opening of the London & Birmingham Railway. The station grew in importance with the opening of the lines to Warwick in 1842 and Nuneaton in 1850.

Now: 4 February 1995
The station at Coventry was rebuilt in the early 1960s and was officially reopened on 1 March 1962, prior to the introduction of electric services over the main line to Birmingham. The station staff assured me that this is exactly the same location. A Class 310 EMU is seen in platform 4. The new island platform and the reorganisation of the tracks occurred during the rebuilding of the station.
A. W. Flowers/Author

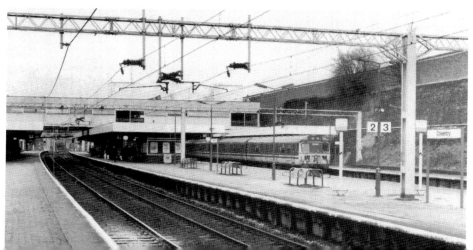

Coventry (west)

Then: 24 December 1959
An up relief to Euston headed by Stanier Class 5 No 45431 enters the station on Christmas Eve.

Now: 4 February 1995
This shot gives a graphic illustration of the changes wrought by the rebuilding of Coventry station. The angle is slightly different to the 'Then' shot as it should, in theory, have been taken from Platform 4, but the Southampton-bound freightliner showed a marked reluctance to move and, after half an hour's wait, I gave up and moved to this platform. The 11.19 Bournemouth-Edinburgh down 'Wessex Scot' is caught in the station. The leading power car is No 43100 *Craigentinny*.
D. Stubbs/Author

Foleshill

Then: 8 September 1963
The line between Coventry and Nuneaton was opened on 12 September 1850. There were six intermediate stations, of which Foleshill was the second out from Coventry. BR Standard Class 4MT No 75035 has just arrived at the station with a workmen's train.

Now: 4 February 1995
The station at Foleshill closed on 18 January 1965, when passenger services over the Leamington Spa-Coventry-Nuneaton route were withdrawn. The route was, however, retained for freight and was reopened to passenger services in two stages: from Leamington to Coventry in 1977 and from Coventry to Nuneaton on 11 May 1987. The present day passenger service is formed of Sprinter units and Class 156 No 156411 is shown passing the site of the station with the 12.16 Coventry-Lincoln service.
A. W. Flowers/Author

Birmingham (New Street)

Then: 10 August 1963
Before rebuilding, this station was a favourite location for photographers. The original station in Birmingham, served by the trains of the London & Birmingham and Grand Junction was situated at Curzon Street (where the impressive station building survives today) and New Street was opened on 1 June 1854. The station was divided between the LNWR and the MR. Here Class 5 No 44685 is shown awaiting departure with a southbound service.

Now: 27 February 1995
Birmingham (New Street) was radically rebuilt in the early 1960s in connection with the electrification of the West Coast main line routes and the construction of a shopping centre. The old building was swept away to be replaced by the austere concrete of the modern age. The station remains one of the most important interchange points on the entire BR network and it is still served by a vast number of trains each day. An ex-Eastern Region Class 309 EMU No 309617, one of a class that was originally constructed for the Clacton electrification, passes through the station on a crew training run prior to entering operation on services from the north.
W. G. Sumner/Author

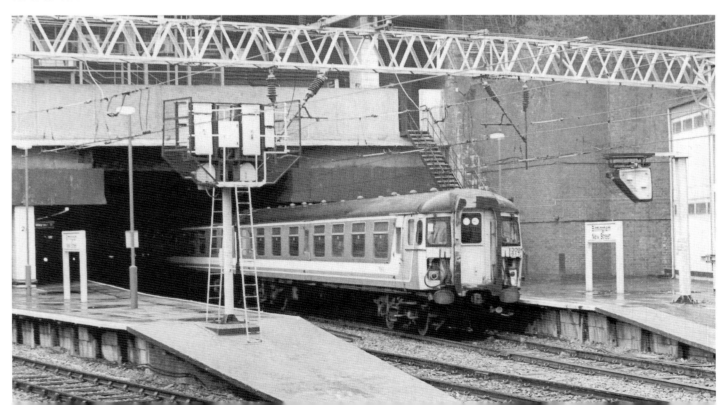

Sutton Coldfield

Then: Undated
Although the line linking Birmingham with Lichfield was first promoted in the 1840s, it was not until 1862 that the route was opened as far as Sutton Coldfield and it took a further 22 years before the line was completed through to Lichfield. Bushbury-allocated Stanier 2-6-2T No 40080 pauses at the station with a local train destined for Birmingham.

Now: 27 February 1995
The station buildings on the down platform have gone along with the water tower on the up, but otherwise the station remains largely unaltered. Detail alterations to note include the improved platform surface and the general tidying up of the platform signs. Work was authorised for the electrification of the cross-city line from Lichfield to Redditch in 1990 and electric services were inaugurated some three years later. Here recently-delivered Class 323 No 323215 passes through the station *en route* for Birmingham.
Ian Allan Library/Author

Four Oaks

Then: June 1949
This is the first station north of Sutton Coldfield on the line towards Lichfield. There are two trains visible; that on the left is heading north, whilst a Stanier 2-6-4T waits in the bay platform with a service for Birmingham.

Now: 27 February 1995
With the exception of the electrification, the station remains largely unchanged. There is the inevitable new footbridge, but the canopied station buildings on this platform survive. The buildings on the down platform have, however, been demolished. Two of the new Hunslet-built Class 323s, Nos 323219 and 323216, pass at the station. The new units were sharing the services with Class 310s and Class 304s on this day.
Ian Allan Library/Author

Winson Green

Then: August 1957
This station was situated on the Stour Valley line just west of Birmingham (New Street). Here we see an up express headed by 'Jubilee' No 45647 *Sturdee* passing through the station.

Now: 4 February 1995
This is not a direct comparison shot — as a result of the station's closure on 16 September 1957 and the consequent inaccessibility of the original location — it does show well the nature of the electrified Stour Valley route. All traces of the station have now gone as Class 86/2 No 86260 *Driver Wallace Oates GC* passes with the 15.55 Birmingham-Liverpool service.
Ian Allan Library/Author

Stafford

Then: Undated
The railways reached Stafford early; it was the major intermediate station when the Grand Junction Railway was opened throughout from Birmingham northwards on 4 July 1837. From those beginnings, the station grew in importance as the number of routes radiated out from it increased. Apart from the ex-LNWR lines to Crewe, Lichfield, Birmingham and Wellington, there was also the ex-Great Northern line towards Uttoxeter. The station clock shows 12.7pm as the down 'Royal Scot' headed by Stanier Pacific No 46240 *City of Coventry*, then allocated to Camden shed, arrives *en route* to Glasgow.

Now: 7 January 1995
Stafford remains an important junction, although the lines to Wellington and Uttoxeter are now but a memory. The station was extensively modernised in connection with the electrification of the West Coast main line; the rebuilt station being officially opened on 31 December 1962. Class 87 No 87031 *Hal 'o the Wynd* passes through the modern station at the head of the 12.30 from Euston to Glasgow.
Ian Allan Library/Author

Great Bridgeford

Then: Undated
This station was situated a few miles north of Stafford on the West Coast main line. An up stopping train is seen calling on the slow line.

Now: 7 January 1995
Passenger services were a relatively early casualty at this station, being withdrawn on 8 August 1949. Freight facilities were to last a decade longer before being withdrawn in June 1959. Today nothing remains of the station as can be seen from this photograph of Class 90 No 90012 *British Transport Police* as it brings up the rear of the 12.45 Liverpool (Lime Street)-Euston service.
Ian Allan Library/Author

Crewe

Then: 20 August 1955

It was under the auspices of the Grand Junction Railway that Crewe was first reached by the railways in 1837. It first achieved junction status in 1840 with the opening of the line to Chester and from that point it grew to become one of the pivotal points on the whole LNWR network. The history of the station and of the railways in the town have been well-documented. Ivatt 2-6-2T No 41229, a Crewe (North)-allocated locomotive for many years, is shown in the north bay ready to leave on the 12.38pm local service to Northwich. The footbridge, which used to cross all the platforms at the north end of the station, was a favourite location for thousands of enthusiasts over the years. It led to North Shed and was usually well guarded during school holidays to deter unofficial visits.

Now: 11 February 1995

The station at Crewe remained largely unchanged from its Victorian layout until a major reconstruction in 1985. Work started on the electrification of the West Coast main line through Crewe in 1959 and the first section, to Liverpool, was energised two years later; public services over the line started on 1 January 1962. The station is still a favourite haunt for enthusiasts, although it lacks the atmosphere of former years and the popular footbridge is long gone. Class 158 No 158756 is ready to leave with the 15.24 service to Bangor, while Class 87/0 No 87022 *Cock o' the North* prepares to leave for Liverpool.

Brian Morrison/Author

Chester (General) (west)

Then: 4 March 1967

The line as far as Saltney Junction opened in 1846 and, as can be seen from the photograph, it was an interesting and complex layout. The Great Western depot used to be on the right of the picture. Stanier Class 5 No 44690 backs out of the station after working the 8.20am service from Paddington, probably to turn on the triangle.

Now: 11 February 1995

The third-rail electrification from Merseyside has now reached Chester and EMU No 508119 is shown leaving with a service northwards. The DMU servicing depot is still in use and the triangle is still used for turning stock. The layout has, however, been much simplified and the volume of traffic is nothing like as heavy as it used to be. The area to the left is now used by the Post Office.

M. Dunnett/Author

Rhyl

Then: Undated

The railways reached Rhyl courtesy of the Chester & Holyhead Railway in 1848 and the station became a busy centre, particularly during the summer months. An engine shed was provided, which served, amongst other duties, the branches to Denbigh and Corwen; this closed in 1963. Stanier Class 5 No 45442 is seen arriving with an express from Manchester to Llandudno, whilst another is visible on ECS work at the carriage shed.

Now: 11 February 1995

The signalbox and a few of the signals still exist, although the track layout has been significantly rationalised. Class 158 No 158756 arrives in the pouring rain on the 09.17 Manchester (Piccadilly)-Holyhead train.

K. Field/Author

Mold

Then: October 1955
This station was situated on the inland alternative route from Chester to the Rhyl-Corwen line at Denbigh. The railways reached the town on 14 August 1849 with the opening of the line from Chester. The line was completed through to Denbigh in 1869. Stanier 2-6-4T No 42461 visited the line with an RCTS special that covered various lines in North Wales.

Now: 11 February 1995
Passenger services between Denbigh and Rhyl were withdrawn on 19 September 1955 (although excursions continued to run until 1961), whilst services were withdrawn from Denbigh to Chester on 30 April 1962. Mold's final link to the railway network disappeared with the closure to freight of the line to Penyffordd on 9 September 1984. Today, although the road overbridge remains, the station has suffered the fate of so many and has been converted into a supermarket and carpark.
Ian Allan Library/Author

Llandudno Junction

Then: 22 June 1963
This is the best known view of the junction. Stanier 'Jubilee' No 45592 *Indore* leaves with an up express. The Chester & Holyhead Railway opened its line from Chester to Bangor to passenger services on 1 May 1848, with services provided by the LNWR. The latter railway bought the C&HR on 1 January 1859. There was no station at Llandudno Junction until the opening of the branch to Llandudno on 1 October 1858; originally it was planned that the branch would leave the main line at Conwy, but it proved impractical to provide junction facilities at that station.

Now: 24 July 1993
As can be seen the track has been rationalised, although the line on the far right has been reinstated following earlier removal. This line is now the usual departure road for up trains. The 14.11 Saturdays Only service from Holyhead to Euston, with InterCity 125 power cars Nos 43125 and 43018, leaves. In the background can be seen the Octel tanks waiting to go forward on the following Monday to Amlych. *Author (2)*

Llandudno Junction Crossing

Then: Undated
The level crossing, combined with the Conwy road bridge and the narrow streets, used to produce incredible traffic jams in the 1950s through to the 1970s. Stanier Class 5 No 45182 heads towards Llandudno probably in the early 1960s.

Now: 9 February 1995
The crossing is now replaced with a bridge and Conwy is now by-passed by a new tunnel under the estuary, whilst the number of trains has declined. Class 153 No 153316, forming the 11.58 from Blaenau Ffestiniog to Llandudno, rounds the sharp curve out of the Junction. The old carriage sheds can be seen in the background; the steam shed was also in the same area. *G. Roberts/Author*

Llandudno

Then: 16 July 1966
The branch to Llandudno opened in October 1858. It was a large station, with extensive carriage sidings, and behind the No 1 signalbox to the left there used to be a turntable and servicing point for those steam locomotives that were not booked for return to Llandudno Junction shed. There was, of course, a considerable number of light engine workings. Stanier Class 5 No 44837 is seen in charge of the 3.25pm Saturdays Only service to Leeds.

Now: 9 February 1995
The hectic activity of the steam era is now very much a thing of the past and locomotive-hauled trains are very much a rarity. The state of the sidings is indicative of the lack of use that they now receive. Class 153 No 153316 heads for the Junction with the 13.26 working to Blaenau Ffestiniog.
J. White/Author

Tal-y-Cafn

Then: Undated
The section of line from Llandudno Junction to Llanrwst was opened on 16 June 1863, but it was not until April 1881 that the branch was completed to Blaenau Ffestiniog. Tal-y-Cafn was the second station out from Llandudno Junction, about half the way to Llanrwst. At the time of this photograph the station was called 'Tal-y-Cafn & Eglwaysbach'; an LNWR 0-6-0 is caught entering the station with a train from Blaenau Ffestiniog.

Now: 9 February 1995
The branch to Blaenau remains open and a single passenger waits to board the single Class 153 unit No 153316 on the 11.58 service from Blaenau to Llandudno. The signalman waits to open the level crossing gates once the train has passed. The station became plain 'Tal-y-Cafn' in 1974.
Ian Allan Library/Author

Betwys-y-Coed

Then: Undated

The section of line between Llanrwst and Betwys-y-Coed opened on 6 April 1868. This was to be the terminus of the branch until the completion of the line to Blaenau Ffestiniog. Stanier 2-6-2T No 40133 has just arrived with a train from Llandudno; it was clearly a popular train given the number of passengers.

Now: 9 February 1995

Although the station building is still standing, the platform canopy has disappeared and the down platform has been demolished. In its place is a railway museum, with small scale running line. Class 153 No 153316 calls with the 15.07 service from Blaenau Ffestiniog to Llandudno; in contrast to the earlier scene there were but two passengers waiting in the pouring rain.

K. Field/Author

Conwy

Then: 28 August 1964

Conway, as it was then spelt, was one of the original stations that opened with the Chester & Holyhead Railway's line to Bangor on 1 May 1848. Always a constricted site, given its position with the castle walls, the station was destined to be overshadowed by Llandudno Junction on the other side of the estuary. This fine picture shows Class 5 No 45003 heading an up parcels service. The station can be seen through the arch.

Now: 9 February 1995

Unfortunately it is not possible to reproduce the 'Then' shot exactly due to the lack of space and height. As can be seen, however, the sidings have been removed. The station was to close on 14 February 1966, but was reopened on 27 June 1987. Class 158 No 158755 passes by at the head of the 13.30 Holyhead-Manchester train. This service had gone over to Class 158 operation from Class 37/4 just a few weeks earlier.

D. Cross/Author

Bangor

Then: 29 August 1963
The railway was completed through from Chester to Bangor on 1 May 1848; the line across to Anglesey via the Britannia Bridge being completed two years later. The Chester & Holyhead Railway became part of the LNWR in 1859. Stanier '8F' No 48749 heads an up freight from Holyhead through the centre road and past Banger No 1 signalbox. On the left there is still plenty of action at the locomotive shed.

Now: 9 February 1995
One can spend a lot of time comparing these two pictures. Whilst the general layout is still basically the same, there are numerous features which have disappeared. The shed continued in use until June 1965 and remains today, albeit in use for industrial purposes. The growth in the trees results in a slightly different angle. The second 'Now' shot records the Crewe test train headed by two Class 47s passing through the centre road; this is one of the few trains still to use this facility.
D. J. Wall/Author (2)

Menai Bridge station

Then: July 1966
Menai Bridge station originally dated from 1858 and was the last station on the North Wales main line before the Britannia Bridge. It was also the junction for the branch to Caernarvon. Stanier Class 5 No 45280 prepares to move some stock to Bangor for a return excursion on a wet day in the summer of 1966; the station at Menai Bridge had closed the previous February.

Britannia Tubular Bridge

Then: Undated
Designed by Robert Stephenson, the Britannia bridge across the Menai Straits between Wales and Anglesey is one of the greatest triumphs of the railway age. The first train to pass over the bridge was on 18 March 1850. This fine photograph of 'Jubilee' No 45603 *Solomon Islands* heading for Holyhead shows the superb structure before the disastrous fire.

Amlwch

Then: Undated
The Act for the construction of the branch from Gaerwen to Amlwch was passed in 1863 and the final section to Amlwch opened to passenger services on 3 June 1867. Although DMUs were introduced on to the line in 1956, steam took over again through to closure.

Now: 9 February 1995
The branch to Caernarvon lost its passenger services, and was closed completely, on 5 January 1970 after having a final swan-song for the investiture of HRH Prince Charles as Prince of Wales the previous year. However, before the track could be lifted, fire had severely damaged the Britannia Bridge and the line to Caernarvon was reopened in June 1970 for freight traffic. It was to close completely again on 31 January 1972 with the reopening of the bridge. Today one has to look very hard for traces of the station, although the remains of the up main platform can be found at the point where the lines disappear from the 'Now' photograph.
E. N. Kneale/Author

Now: 9 February 1995
Today, the view is spoilt by the road built over the bridge which was opened in July 1980. The bridge had survived for almost 150 years when, on 23/24 May 1970, it was almost destroyed by fire. Following rebuilding, the bridge was load tested on 18 January 1972 and services resumed shortly thereafter. As can be seen the line across the bridge has been singled, although the two lions remain.
P. Ransome-Wallis/Author

Now: 9 February 1995
Passenger services over the line ceased on 7 December 1964 and, as can be seen, the station area has been largely cleared with the exception of the goods shed. The branch to Amlwych, however, remained open for freight traffic to the Associated Octel factory — which is situated at the end of a ³/₄-mile extension to the branch off to the right of this photograph — until this traffic ceased in 1994. There has been a campaign to restore passenger services over the line, although nothing definite has been announced at the time of writing.
Ian Allan Library/Author

Warrington Arpley Junction

Then: 27 September 1967
This junction was located just to the east of Warrington and provided a link between the ex-LNWR line from Manchester to Liverpool via Warrington and Speke and the West Coast main line from Weaver Junction northwards. Stanier '8F' No 48119 heads towards Liverpool with a freight. The lines in the right foreground head towards the West Coast route. By this date the route was already freight-only, passenger services between Ditton and Timperley having been withdrawn on 10 September 1962.

Now: 30 January 1995
The background has altered although the layout remains remarkably unchanged. The goods shed has gone but the signalbox remains. The line from Latchford (just east of this location) eastwards to Skelton Junction closed completely on 8 July 1985. The line remains to allow merry-go-round trains to Fiddlers Ferry power station to reverse. Class 56 No 56037 *Richard Trevithick* has just reversed and is now heading towards the power station. In the background is the stabling point and sister locomotives Nos 56036 and 56009 can be seen.
J. H. Cooper-Smith/Author

Winwick Junction (north)

Then: 4 September 1960
A diverted Liverpool-Birmingham express comes off the line from Earlestown headed by Stanier 'Jubilee' class No 45681 *Aboukir*. In the background the West Coast main line can be seen heading off to the right, whilst the famous Vulcan Foundry, builder of many railway locomotives, can be seen in the background.

Now: 30 January 1995
The signalbox has gone as Class 150/1 No 150201 in Merseyrail livery passes under the wires forming the 14.57 Liverpool-Ellesmere Port service. Although it is many years since a locomotive emerged from the foundry, the building remains although it has lost its rooftop legend.
Ian Allan Library/Author

Winwick Junction (south)

Then: 29 September 1962
Stanier Pacific No 46237 *City of Bristol* performs a lowly task as it heads a Crewe-Carlisle goods train. The signals indicate that it is about to take the West Coast main line northwards. The railway at arrived Winwick when the Grand Junction opened throughout to join the Liverpool & Manchester at Newton (just north of this point). It became a junction when the line to Golbourne Junction opened on 1 August 1864. There was originally a Grand Junction station here, but it closed as early as 28 November 1840. The actual junction is on the other side of the bridge behind the photographer

Now: 30 January 1995
Two views of Winwick Junction have been included as it was a popular location for photographs during the steam era; electrification has, however, ruined it although the bridge in the background can still provide a reasonable viewing point. Class 158 No 158752 passes the junction on the 13.53 Llandudno-Manchester (Piccadilly) service.
J. R. Carter/Author

Cheadle Hulme

Then: 9 October 1954
This is the location of the point where the lines to Crewe and Stoke diverge just south of Stockport. Stanier 'Jubilee' class No 45553 *Canada* heads the 12.5pm Manchester (London Road)-Stoke-Euston service. The photograph was taken from the station footbridge.

Stockport Edgeley

Then May 1957
Although the railways reached Stockport courtesy of the Manchester & Birmingham Railway in 1840 when the section from Manchester to the town opened, it was not until 15 February 1843 that the present station was opened. The temporary station survived as Heaton Norris until 1959. The line opened south of Stockport to Sandbach in 1842. This is a general view of the station taken prior to the electrification of the line between Crewe and Manchester.

Heaton Norris (Stockport)

Then: Undated
Prior to electrification at the end of the 1950s, this junction, just to the west of Stockport Edgeley, had a very impressive array of semaphore signals. An unidentified Stanier Class 5 heads a rake of ex-LNER stock in BR livery towards Manchester.

Now: 30 January 1995
The station footbridge is now a thing of the past, no doubt removed due to electrification, and the 'Now' photograph is consequently taken from platform level. It shows InterCity Class 47 No 47843 heading the 11.17 Manchester (Piccadilly)-Birmingham train. The signalbox still stands, although the steps seem to have moved from one side to the other.
D. J. Beaver/Author

Now: 30 January 1995
As can be seen from the position of the church spire in the background, it was not possible to replicate the original photographer's position exactly. However, the layout of this busy station has not altered greatly over the past 40 years despite the arrival of the 25kV electrification. The carriage shed, which was situated on the extreme left of the 'Then' photograph, has gone, although the area is still used for the stabling of EMUs and DMUs. The area in the foreground is now a car park. A Class 101 DMU of Regional Railways departs from the station.
T. Lewis/Author

Now: 5 February 1995
The station at Heaton Norris closed on 2 March 1959. Class 87 No 87015 *Howard of Effingham* passes on the 11.10 service from Euston to Manchester Piccadilly.
Nigel Dyckhoff/Author

Disley

Then: Undated
This is one of the intermediate stations between Stockport and Buxton on the ex-LNWR line. This route opened between Stockport and Whaley Bridge, under the aegis of the Stockport, Disley & Whaley Bridge Railway, on 9 June 1857. The extension from Whaley Bridge to Buxton opened on 15 June 1864 and two years later the SD&WBR was vested in the LNWR. Class 5 No 45096 passes the signalbox hauling a ECS working to Buxton to form a special to Blackpool.
Now: 2 February 1995
The line remains open to passenger services and currently possesses an hourly service. Class 150/2 No 150201 in Merseyrail livery approaches the station on the 10.27 Blackpool-Buxton service. The signalbox still stands, although it is unmanned and has lost its nameboard.
K. Field/Author

Buxton

Then: July 1955

The town of Buxton was served by lines built by both the Midland and LNWR; inevitably this meant two stations, although externally both stations were very similar. The Midland was the first to arrive on 1 June 1866 with the LNWR line following later the same month. The Midland route was closed on 3 March 1966, leaving the ex-LNWR line to Manchester as the town's sole passenger link. Fowler 2-6-4T No 42366, from a class extensively used on the Manchester trains, waits to leave with a stopping train.

Now: 11 January 1995

Although the station layout and buildings have been rationalised, the dramatic window remains. The services to Manchester are now entirely in the hands of Sprinters and Class 150/1 No 150146 is seen ready to depart. Whilst facilities in the area have declined, there remains a number of freight-only lines serving the limestone industry and Buxton still retains a depot for the servicing of locomotives used on this traffic.

Ian Allan Library/Author

Thrapston Bridge Street

Then: 11 April 1964

The Northamptonshire town of Thrapston possessed two railway stations, one on the ex-LNWR line from Northampton to Peterborough and one on the ex-Midland line from Kettering to Huntingdon. Stanier Mogul No 42945, the first of the class to be built, calls at the station with the 3.50pm service from Peterborough a few weeks before closure.

Now: 14 January 1995

Passenger services over the line were withdrawn on 4 May 1964 and freight services a year later. The fine station has now completely disappeared and the site is occupied by a timber company. This picture was taken by kind permission of the director.

M. Mitchell/Author

Thorpe

Then: 25 April 1964
This was the next station along the ex-LNWR line from Northampton to Peterborough. Fairburn 2-6-4T No 42062 arrives with the 3.50pm service from Peterborough to Northampton.

Rockingham

Then: 18 May 1964
From Yarwell Junction, near Peterborough, it was possible to travel south towards Northampton or west, through Rockingham, towards Market Harborough and thence again towards Northampton or Rugby. Stanier Class 5 No 44915 is pictured arriving with the 12.40pm service from Harwich Town to Rugby.

Wigston Glen Parva Junction

Then: 28 June 1965
The line from Nuneaton to Wigston provided the LNWR with access to Leicester over the metals of the Midland Railway. It opened from Nuneaton to Hinckley on 1 January 1862 and thence to Wigston on 1 January 1864. Stanier '8F' No 48699 is pictured heading a westbound coal train as it approaches Wigston Glen Parva station over the Leicester line. The line to the right provided the third arm of the triangle and connected with the Midland main line southwards Kettering. The original station at this point closed on 4 March 1968.

Now: 14 January 1995
The station, like that at Thrapston, was closed to passenger services on 4 May 1964 but unlike the previous station Thorpe remains. It has been converted into a superb residence with the trackbed converted into a lawn. I am grateful to the owner of the house for permission to take this illustration. Although the line has long gone, two sections remain; in Peterborough the line from the town through to Wansford and Yarwell Junction now forms the preserved Nene Valley Railway, whilst in Northampton a stub remains to serve a number of freight terminals in the town.
M. Mitchell/Author

Now: 22 January 1995
The line lost its passenger services on 6 June 1966 and today the station has been converted into a private house and the road crosses behind the fence where once there was a level crossing. Note the name still visible on the house side. Again I am grateful for permission from the owner to take this photograph from his garden.
G. D. King/Author

Now: 23 January 1995
A new station called Wigston South, situated on the curve, opened on 10 May 1986. It is situated some 400yd closer to Leicester as this picture of Sprinter No 156407 shows. The train was the 15.03 Birmingham-Leicester service.
M. Mitchell/Author

Manchester Exchange

Then: 24 August 1968
A Class 124 Trans Pennine set on a Liverpool-Hull working passes under the fine overall roof at Exchange station. A Class 101 Metro-Cammell DMU on the left awaits departure for Chester. This extremely fine station was built in 1884 and remained in use until May 1969. The tracks continued in use as through lines for several years, whilst the overall roof was gradually demolished and the platform space utilised for car parking.

Now: 11 December 1994
The site of this once proud station is now all but cleared. With the modernisation and rationalisation at Victoria — to which Exchange was linked by a through platform — the tracks have been removed and the buildings completely demolished. On the far right are visible the Victoria-Salford lines over which services continue to operate to and from the new Victoria.
Author (2)

Manchester (Oxford Road)

Then: Undated
This is an official photograph taken at the time of the station's rebuilding and features one of the then new Class AM4/2 (Class 304) EMUs. The station was rebuilt from 1959 onwards.

Now: 2 February 1995
Thirty-five years on and little has changed. There is more clutter on the platforms and the platforms have been renumbered. On the Sunday that the 'Now' photograph was taken, the line through the station was closed for engineering work and so it was impossible to get a picture of a train in the platform.

Ian Allan Library/Author

Oldham, Ashton & Guide Bridge Junction

Then: undated
Fairburn design 2-6-4T No 42696 heads towards Oldham Clegg Street with a parcels service from Manchester. This line was part of the Oldham, Ashton-under-Lyne & Guide Bridge Joint, which was controlled by the LNWR and the Great Central.
Now: 26 November 1994
The line to Oldham Clegg Street lost its passenger services on 4 May 1959 and was to close completely on 20 May 1967. Since the earlier photograph was taken the overbridge at this point has been demolished and a replacement signalbox built, which controls the junction to the now little-used line round to Ashton Moss. A Class 142 heads towards the box with the 11.24 from Wakefield to Manchester.
J. Davenport/Author

Stalybridge

Then: 27 April 1968
One of the many specials that ran in the last months of main line steam on British Railways is heading over the Pennines hauled by a couple of Patricroft-based BR Standard Class 5s Nos 73050 and 73069. The former was to escape the scrapman and is currently preserved on the Nene Valley Railway in Peterborough. The lines on the left of the photograph were the ex-LNWR lines to Diggle via Micklehurst, which had lost their passenger services on 7 September 1964, that ran parallel with the main line towards Standedge. The train is about to enter Stalybridge Tunnel.
Now: 26 November 1994
Although the signalbox has been replaced, the junction with the Micklehurst line lifted and some of the mill chimneys on the skyline have vanished, the signal closest to the camera remains unchanged as Pacer No 142036 leaves on the 11.55 Manchester-Wakefield service.
Author (2)

Mossley

Then: Undated
A holiday extra special passes Mossley headed by Stanier Class 5 No 45201 on the Micklehurst route.
Now: 26 November
This route was closed completely in October 1966 and, as can be seen, there are only the bridge abutments to show that the line passed this site.
K. Field/Author

Lydgate Tunnel Grasscroft

Then: Undated
Fowler 2-6-2T No 40059 emerges from the tunnel *en route* to Delph from Oldham. The train was a push-pull working known locally as the 'Delph Donkey'. The service from Oldham Clegg Street called at Oldham Glodwick Street, Lees, Grotton & Springhead, Grasscroft, Greenfield, Moorgate, Dobcross and Delph. Journey times were around the half hour for the 6¾ mile journey — an average speed of some 15mph.
Now: 28 November 1994
Passenger services were withdrawn on 2 May 1955 and the section of line from Oldham to the junction with the main line at Greenfield closed completely on 10 April 1964. As can be seen, nature has now taken over and even in late autumn the tunnel mouth is invisible.
J. Davenport/Author

Saddleworth-Diggle

Then: 2 July 1967
The lines to the left were the former Micklehurst loop, which had been closed completely for almost a year when 'Britannia' No 70038 *Robin Hood* headed east with a Stephenson Locomotive Society special. The stations on the loop line had closed as early as 1916. In the background can be seen the short Butterhouse Tunnel.
Now: 29 November 1994
Although the name of the factory seems to have changed in the past quarter of a century and the closed Micklehurst loop has been lifted, much of the scene is unchanged as Sprinter No 156486 heads east on the 11.34 Manchester Piccadilly-Hull service.
Author (2)

Diggle

Then: Mid-1950s

Situated at the western end of the Standedge Tunnels, Diggle station opened in August 1949. The original single-bore tunnel was built between 1846 and 1849 followed by the second between 1868 and 1870. Increasing traffic in the latter years of the century resulted in the twin north tunnel being constructed between 1890 and 1894. The new tunnel was 3 miles 64yd long, two yards longer than the single bores.

Diggle possessed a busy goods yard as can be seen. An ex-WD 2-8-0 is in the up yard, as 'Jubilee' No 45593 *Kolhapur* passes on the up fast line prior to taking the Micklehurst loop. On the left of the picture the third train is heading over the line via Greenfield.

Now: 14 October 1994

The station closed in October 1963. Everything has now vanished except the signalbox and the down loop. Class 60 No 60066 *John Logie Baird* heads the Greater Manchester Council empty refuse train from Roxby to Northenden.
Ian Allan Library/Author

Marsden

Then: Late 1950s
Situated at the eastern end of the 5,344yd-long Standedge Tunnel, this station opened in August 1849. Stockport-based Fowler 2-6-4T No 42379 passes the station on a Manchester-Leeds stopping train. The local trains used to stop in platform 2 and then set back and cross over to the down line to return to Leeds. The loop line then had a platform added to allow the express trains to pass.

Golcar

Then: 20 June 1959
The station, opened in 1849 is situated nearly halfway up the bank from Huddersfield to Marsden. As can be seen in the picture of Edge Hill (8A) allocated Class 5 No 44772, which is leaving on a Leeds-Manchester stopping traint. Traffic over these lines did not seem to follow any definite pattern between freight and passenger services. However, reduction in trans-Pennine freight services allowed for the lifting of two lines in 1966 and the closure of the twin-bore tunnels at Standedge. Slaithwaite station, two miles further towards Manchester, was opened and closed on the same day as Golcar, but was reopened in December 1992.

Gledholt

Then: 24 May 1959
At the west end of Gledholt Tunnel, the four tracks of the main line used to run alongside sidings. These normally housed carriages which, after the war, seldom seemed to move except at summer weekends. There was also a signalbox to control the crossovers between the fast and slow lines. A Manchester (London Road)-Marylebone express, which had been diverted off the Woodhead route, is shown approaching the tunnel with very unusual motive power for the area in the form of Gorton-allocated Gresley 'K3' 2-6-0 No 61865, which was replaced by a Stanier Class 5 at Huddersfield as the train reversed and took the Penistone line to regain its original route.

Now: 28 November 1994
The station has avoided closure. As can be seen as Pacer No 142045 arrives with the 10.25 service from Wakefield, there have been considerable alterations to the buildings. The current hourly service runs through from Wakefield to Manchester.
K. Field/Author

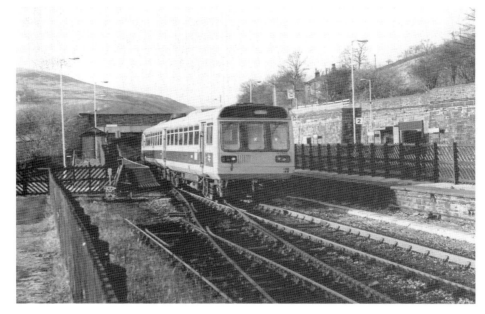

Now: 1 November 1994
The station at Golcar closed on 7 October 1968. Today the Class 158s rush past the site of the station at 90mph on the remaining double track and the trees are starting to encroach on the remains of the old trackbed. Unit No 158775 is heading for Huddersfield on the 12.22 Liverpool-York service.
Author (2)

Now: 1 November 1994
Today only two tracks remain and the land formerly occupied by the sidings seems to have been recently sold for development. The 12.28 Manchester Airport-York service is shown, formed of Class 158 No 158809.
Author (2)

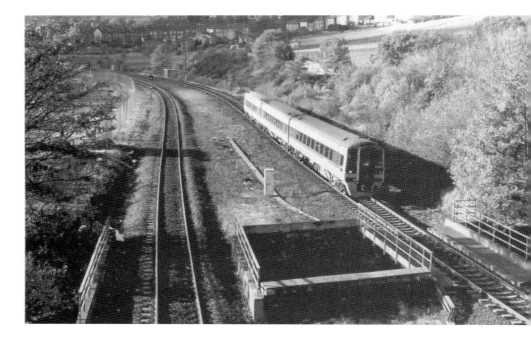

Huddersfield

Then: Mid-1950s
The east end bay platforms of the station were used by the local services to Wakefield, Halifax, Cleckheaton and other trains which operated on the erstwhile L&YR metals. In the background is Fitzwilliam Street goods depot. The platform to the right of the locomotives usually served the through services to Leeds, the large water tower being available for the locomotives to be replenished. Shown are two '2MT' Standard tanks, Nos 84014 and 84105, which together with others were allocated new to Low Moor shed for local services in 1953.

Now: December 1994
Today the bay still exists, but the platforms have been reduced in length as these two Pacer units, parked up on a Sunday, show. The large warehouse behind the trains is still in use. Huddersfield station, which opened in 1847 (although the station building was not completed until 1850), is one of the finest in the country. The neo-classical structure, designed by J. P. Pritchett, is a listed building and has recently been cleaned externally.
Author (2)

Bradley

Then: 4 June 1966
Ex-Crosti boilered Standard Class 9F 2-10-0 No 92020 trundles past the site of Bradley station with an up freight. Opened in August 1847, the station survived until March 1950. In the background is Bradley Junction, which formed a triangle with the ex-L&YR Calder Valley route; the other junction being at Heaton Lodge.

Now: 2 March 1994
There are now only two tracks which carry the intensive service to Huddersfield. The Greater Manchester Council rubbish train was diagrammed to fit in between the Sprinter-operated passenger services. The locomotive is Class 60 No 60016 *Langdale Pike*, which is returning to Manchester from Roxby near Scunthorpe. The track towards the Calder Valley line are still *in situ* as there are hopes that one day the Bradford-Halifax-Huddersfield service may be reinstated.

Author (2)

Bradley Junction

Then: 20 July 1962
The previous shot at Bradley looked eastward; in contrast this illustration portrays the scene looking towards Huddersfield as rebuilt 'Patriot' No 45540 *Sir Robert Turnbull* passes on the 9.30am Saturdays Only summer service from Manchester to Leeds City.
Now: 13 March 1994
By contrast, the Redland ballast train is seen in operation at the junction, when the track was being relaid in order to increase the speed limit. Class 60 No 60010 *Punlumon/Plynlimon* provides the motive power.
Author (2)

Mirfield Shed

Then: 12 May 1961
This location is in fact the nearest vantage point to view trains from the author's home since 1963 and many hours have been spent here over the past years. Visits to the location in the days of steam were infrequent, but did result in a number of photographs. This busy scene shows the Heaton-Red Bank Vans, headed by two Stanier Class 5s Nos 44735 and 44895, passing an Austerity 2-8-0 and 2-6-0 'Crab' No 42789 on the shed.

Proposals for a shed first appeared in 1849, but it was not until 1885 that the present depot, which still stands today, was completed. Between these dates there were many inadequate developments. Mirfield was one of the last steam sheds to close in the area, finally succumbing in April 1967.

Now: 15 November 1994
Today the track layout has been reduced to three through lines, over which runs a continuous procession of Sprinters and Pacers interspersed with some freight Class 158 No 158779 is pictured working the 13.18 Hull-Manchester Piccadilly service. It is worth comparing the skyline of the two pictures, which show how the traditional woollen industry has vanished over the past 30 years.
Author (2)

Mirfield station

Then: 19 September 1966
Holbeck-based 'Jubilee' No 45593, formerly named *Kolhapur*, is in the bay at the west end of the station collecting a van to attach to the afternoon Leeds-Wavertree train. The station was opened in April 1845.

Now: 18 December 1994
The station remains in use, although the bay has now been filled in and bushes planted. The old station buildings were demolished and replaced by the familiar bus shelter. Class 158 No 158806 is pictured entering the station. The train is about to stop as it was being diverted via the Calder Valley route due to engineering work over the Standedge line. The westbound stopping trains now use the platform on the slow line visible just to the right-hand side of the train. This allows the express trains to overtake between Thornhill and Heaton Lodge junctions.
Author (2)

Morley (Low)

Then: 10 June 1966
Opened in 1845, the station received the suffix 'Low' to differentiate it from 'High', which was situated on the ex-Great Northern Railway line between Bradford and Wakefield. The station is situated at the east end of the 3,369yd-long Morley Tunnel and the summit of the climb out of Leeds is to be found in the tunnel. Unusual motive power for the famous Heaton-Red Bank van train is '8F' No 48080, which was struggling with its 22-van load. The train was normally double-headed so no doubt the Farnley Junction '8F' was covering for a failure.

Earlestown

Then: 28 August 1964
The Liverpool & Manchester Railway, one of the great names in Britain's railway history, opened in 1830. Earlestown is situated about halfway along the line and is the point where the line from Warrington joins the L&MR. The 12.10pm service from Hull leaves for Manchester. To the right a Warrington-St Helens (Shaw Street) service, formed of a two-car DMU, is in platform No 4, whilst the 3pm Liverpool-Newcastle service is just leaving from behind the service from Hull.

Lancaster (Castle)

Then: 26 August 1954
The railways reached Lancaster with the opening of the Lancaster & Preston Junction Railway on 25 June 1840. Here an up express freight headed by Carlisle Upperby-allocated Stanier Class 5 No 44939 passes through the centre road. On the right are the electrified lines of the Lancaster-Morecambe-Heysham route of the former Midland Railway dropping down to Lancaster (Green Ayre) station.

Now: 2 November 1994
Although shorn of the 'Low' following the
closure of the ex-GNR lines, Morley remains
open to passenger services. Today, however,
the sidings, signalbox and station buildings
have gone, whilst there are probably more
trains than ever before using the line. One of
the three-car Class 158s, No 158814,
approaches the station on the 12.13
Middlesbrough-Manchester Airport service.
Author (2)

Now: 11 February 1995
Although there has been some
rationalisation, particularly with the line
towards Warrington, the station is
remarkably unchanged. Class 150/1
No 150148 is ready to leave with the 16.24
service to Liverpool. It was so dark on this
occasion that the picture need a one-second
exposure at f5.6 on 400ASA film; hence it
was taken with the train still static in the
station.
E. N. Bellass/Author

Now: 24 January 1995
Passenger services over the line to Green
Ayre were withdrawn in 1966 and the
background has altered considerably as Res-
liveried Class 86/2 No 86210 *CIT 75th
Anniversary* passes with what appears to be a
very uneconomical working.
R. H. Leslie/Author

Hest Bank

Then: 19 July 1958
This was a favourite location amongst railway enthusiasts in the age of steam to watch expresses running over the West Coast main line. Caprotti valve gear-fitted Stanier Class 5 No 44745 pilots Fowler 2-6-4T No 42317 on an up Barrow-Preston service.
Now:
Everything has now changed. The station was closed on 3 February 1969 and has been demolished. The signalbox for controlling the level crossing has moved to the north side of the road and a new footbridge built. A Regional Railways-liveried Class 144 No 144012 rushes past the site at its maximum speed working the 13.01 Leeds-Lancaster service.
F. Wilde/Author

Preston station

Then: 24 July 1965
Although the railways reached Preston from the south with the opening of the North Union Railway on 31 October 1838 and from the north with the opening on 25 June 1840 of the Lancaster & Preston Junction Railway, the train shed that stands today was built in 1880. In style it is typical of many constructed by the LNWR, of which only a few examples remain largely intact. The 1880 building makes Preston an impressive building and the railways remain busy in the area. Seen under the overall roof. Stanier Class 5 No 44846 arrives with a Saturday relief from Manchester to Blackpool.

Carnforth Yard

Then: 2 June 1968
Although taken before the closure of the shed to main line steam, on 5 August 1968, a number preserved locomotives were already being kept in the yard. These included the two Fairburn 2-6-4Ts, which are now displayed at the Lakeside & Haverthwaite Railway, Ivatt 2-6-0 No 6441, which is still resident but currently on an extensive main line tour, and Thompson 'B1' No 1306. In the distance the freight yard was still very active.
Now: 22 December 1994
This comparison shows that even in preservation sites can change. A Midland Railway pattern signalbox has appeared and the platform for the steam centre's demonstration line has been constructed. Reflecting the decline in freight, the yard has become a car park serving the railway museum. *Author (2)*

Now: 6 January 1995
This part of the station has changed very little over the past 30 years and even the overhead catenary seems remarkably unobtrusive. On a much quieter day in January Pacer unit No 142013 has just arrived to form the 12.26 service to Blackpool South.
Ron Fisher/Author

Windermere

Then: 2 August 1968
The branch from Oxenholme opened in April 1847 to passenger services. It was a particularly busy line, especially during the summer months. Seen at the terminus on 2 August 1968 is Stanier Class 5 No 44709 operating, as can be seen from the chalked slogans on the smokebox, the last BR steam working over the branch. In the distance a Type 2 (later Class 25) awaits departure with a passenger train.

Now: 22 December 1994
Over the past quarter of a century traffic has gradually declined and the route has been singled and run-round facilities have been removed. Services are now operated by Sprinters. The yard on this site is now occupied by Lakeland Plastics, whilst the one that used to be on the other side is a car park for a supermarket. The second 'Now' illustration shows Sprinter No 156427 in the remaining platform ready to depart with a service for Manchester Airport.
J. Scrace/Author (2)

Staveley

Then: 2 August 1968
This is one of three intermediate stations on the Windermere branch — the others being Kendal and Burneside — and we see again the last steam-operated train over the branch being hauled by 'Black 5' No 44709.
Now: 22 December 1994
The double-track line and attractive station building are things of the past as the surviving single line and bus shelter testify. I arrived just 10min before the train was scheduled with passengers waiting on the platform; unfortunately, two minutes before the train was due a taxi arrived and took them away. Apparently a points failure had caused the train to be cancelled.
J. Scrace/Author

Oxenholme (south)

Then: 6 August 1966
A busy scene at the side of the locomotive depot shows a very dirty 'Britannia' No 70028, formerly named *Royal Star*, on a down express. In the loop a track train, headed by two Stanier '8Fs', awaits the road. The shed can be seen on the right-hand side. Construction of the shed was authorised in 1846 and it was rebuilt in 1880 with a capacity of 12 locomotives. The shed's main duties were the provision of banking and piloting locomotives to Shap Summit.
Now: 14 February 1995
The shed finally closed in June 1962 and the site has been subsequently cleared. Passing the surviving loops the down 'Devon Scot', the 07.25 from Plymouth to Aberdeen, heads north towards the station formed of an InterCity 125 with power cars Nos 43162/43153.
Author (2)

Oxenholme station

Then: 6 August 1966
The station at Oxenholme opened in July 1846 and it was the junction for the branch to Kendal and Windermere. BR Standard '9F' 2-10-0 No 92056 drifts through the station and past No 2 signalbox on its way south. The branch platform can be seen to the left of the station.

Now: 14 February 1995
Access to the branch used to be gained just north of the station, as well as from the south end, but the north points have now been removed. Through the overhead lines of the West Coast main line it is possible to see that the station has not changed much. Inevitably, there has been a reduction in the sidings. Class 87 No 87014 *Knight of the Thistle* leaves with the 11.40 service from Glasgow to Euston.
Author (2)

Grayrigg

Then: 16 August 1958
This isolated station on the West Coast main line north of Oxenholme closed to passenger services on 1 February 1954, but freight facilities continued until 1960. 'Jubilee' No 45705 *Seahorse* makes slow progress on a down express.

Now: 14 February 1995
Although the station has been demolished, the loops remain to enable passenger trains to overtake freight services. In contrast to the slow-moving 'Jubilee' class 86/2 No 86260 *Driver Wallace GC* will have slowed for the 80mph restriction around the curve. It was not possible to achieve exactly the same elevation as in the 'Then' shot.
Author (2)

Tebay Shed

Then: 16 August 1958
The Fowler 2-6-4Ts were used as bankers up Shap for at least two decades and the two illustrated here, Nos 42396 and 42404, were allocated to Tebay for some time. The original shed was modernised with a new roof in 1947 and a new coal and ash plant was installed in 1956. The shed was supplied with a new 60ft turntable at the same time. Its final allocation comprised five BR Standard Class 4MT 4-6-0s before closure on 1 January 1968.
Now: 14 February 1995
After closure the shed was demolished and nothing now remains except for the cottages which were built to house railwaymen.
Author (2)

Tebay

Then: Undated
The line through Tebay to Carlisle was formally opened on 15 December 1846 under the auspices of the Lancaster & Carlisle Railway. The town's importance as a railway centre grew in 1861 with the opening of the South Durham & Lancashire Union Railway from Bishop Auckland. The picture of Bank Hall-allocated 'Jubilee' No 45717 *Dauntless* was probably taken in the late 1950s and shows the locomotive working a Glasgow-Liverpool express. It was taken from the station footbridge. The shed was on the left and the ex-North eastern Railway yards can be seen on the right.
Now: 14 February 1995
No elevation is available today to show the current scene as an unidentified Class 90 heads north on the 08.15 Euston-Glasgow service. Passenger services over the ex-NER line to Kirkby Stephen were withdrawn on 3 December 1952, whilst freight was to succumb a decade later on 22 January 1962
Ian Allan Library/Author

Penrith

Then: 18 August 1962
Penrith was once a busy junction on the West Coast main line, with lines heading west to Keswick and east to Kirkby Stephen. The town also possessed a small shed, which opened in 1864/65 and housed the locomotives used on the NER route. It was closed on 18 June 1962 and can be clearly seen behind an up express headed by 'Jubilee' class No 45572 *Eire*. The locomotive was at this time allocated to Shrewsbury and the train a Perth-Manchester express.

Now: 19 January 1995
Little now remains from the 'Then' shot; even the excellent vantage point is a thing of the past. The loop does, however, remain as an InterCity 125, with power cars Nos 43086 and 43087, departs at 09.56 with the 06.50 up 'Wessex Scot' from Edinburgh.
Derek Cross/Author

Carlisle

Then: Undated

Once Carlisle was host to seven different pre-Grouping railway companies and, in steam days, must have been one of the best centres in the country for the enthusiast. No doubt many took photographs from this location; this particular shot probably dates from the early 1960s and shows 'Princess Royal' No 46204 *Princess Louise* ready to depart with an up express whilst local 'Jinty' No 47292 shunts empty stock.

Now: 5 December 1994

Fortunately the station has altered little except for the electrification of the line, although elsewhere in Carlisle the changes have been radical. Class 47 No 47746 is ready to depart at 20.30 with an up mail service.

Ian Allan Library/Author

North London Railway

The North London Railway was originally promoted in the 1840s as the East & West India Docks & Birmingham Junction Railway, with the intention of providing a link between Camden and the docks. The first section of the line, between Islington and Bow Junction, opened on 26 September 1850. It was then further extended westwards until it reached Hampstead Road (now Primrose Hill) on 9 June 1851. On 1 January 1852 the line was further extended from Bow to Poplar.

The company changed its name to the North London Railway on 1 January 1853. The company had close links with the London & North Western Railway, and provided services over the LNWR line west of Primrose Hill; it was not, however, until 1922 that the company was completely absorbed by its larger partner.

Sole access to the city was obtained on 1 November 1865 with the opening of the line from Dalston to a new terminus at Broad Street, adjacent to the Great Eastern's terminus at Liverpool Street; prior to that date the North London had used Fenchurch Street station.

At the Grouping in 1923, the North London, as part of the LNWR, passed to the LMS. The first casualty occurred on 14 May 1944 when the passenger services over the line from Dalston Junction to Poplar were withdrawn (although a replacement bus service operated until the following year). The line from Victoria Park Junction (on the Dalston-Stratford line) to Poplar was completely closed from October 1983; ironically, the section south of Bow now forms part of the new Docklands Light Railway.

The next major change to affect the ex-North London lines occurred on 30 June 1986 when Broad Street station was finally closed, along with the line to Dalston Junction) and the remaining services transferred to Liverpool Street via a new curve. North London line services now run from Dalston to North Woolwich via the reopened Dalston Junction-Stratford line. There are, however, proposals which could seen trains restored to part of the old Dalston Junction-Broad Street line, if current plans for the extension of the East London Line of London Underground from Shoreditch come to fruition.

Bow Works

Then: 16 May 1955
Bow Works was built by the North London Railway in 1853 and remained active repairing steam locomotives until closure in 1960. A view inside the works shows LMS 'Jinty' No 47487 under repair together with another member of the class and some ex-LT&SR 4-4-2Ts.
Now: January 1995
The comparison today is dramatic as the site of the works has been taken over by a residential estate. Where once locomotives were repaired is now the ground floor of a block of flats where the heating boiler and other items of building maintenance are kept behind locked doors.
Brian Morrison (2)

South Bromley

Then: Undated
The North London line from Bow to Poplar, on which this station was situated, opened on 1 January 1852. Passenger services were withdrawn between Poplar and Dalston Junction on 15 April 1944 (although a replacement bus service ran until 23 April 1945).

Now: 18 January 1995
Freight services survived over the line after closure to passenger services until 3 October 1983. The section north of Bow to Victoria Park Junction was closed completely, but the track south of Bow was utilised as part of the new Docklands Light Railway. All traces of the old station have disappeared, but one square building remains in the distance to provide a reference between the two views. Two of the DLR's B90 stock, Nos 33 and 30, head south past the site of the old station.
Ian Library/Brian Morrison

Devons Road Shed

Then: 8 October 1955
The shed on the site, coded 1D by BR, was opened in 1882. Ex-Somerset & Dorset Joint Railway 'Jinty' Class 3F No 47315 is shown on shed.
Now:
The shed remained in use until 1964, but was to become the first all-diesel shed on BR in 1958. It was, however, used to store steam locomotives until 1963. Today a warehouse building now stands on the site, and a Daihatsu 'Tonka Toy' has replaced the more elegant-looking 'Jinty'.
Brian Morrison (2)

Broad Street

Then: 1925
A gap of 70 years separates these two views. Broad Street was the North London's terminus and was situated on the north side of Liverpool Street station. It opened to passenger traffic, following completion of an expensive extension, on 1 November 1865. Such was the success of the line that the route from Dalston Broad Street was quadrupled by 1874. Close examination of the photograph shows that there are four of the NLR's tank locomotives present.
Now: 18 January 1995
Following construction of a new link at Dalston, services were diverted away from Broad Street to Liverpool Street after the closure of the line from Dalston Junction on 27 June 1986. The closure was to facilitate construction of one of the largest office developments in London — the Broadgate complex. The new offices have completely obliterated all trace of the Italianate station. Situated at the end of the platforms, from where the 1925 photograph was taken, is now one of the many buildings that occupy the site.
Ian Allan Library/Brian Morrison

Poplar station

Then: 5 May 1956
Although closed more than a decade before the date of this photograph, at least one of the platforms of this station survived when ex-NLR 0-6-0T No 58859 hauled an LCGB rail tour through the station. Designed by the NLR's second Locomotive Superintendent, J. C. Park, No 58859 was one of a batch introduced in 1879. One of the class, No 58850, survives in preservation after having spent its later years well away from its traditional haunts.

Now: 18 January 1995
Following the complete closure of the line in 1983, the line was taken over to form part of the new Docklands Light Railway and DLR All Saints station now occupies the site of the ex-NLR station. With the chimney, fire station clock tower and a number of other buildings in the background still extant, two of the DLR's P89 stock, Nos 14 and 17, form a service from Stratford to Canary Wharf.
R. E. Vincent/Brian Morrison

Cromford & High Peak Railway

The C&HPR was one of the earliest railways built to feature in this book. Its first Act dated from 2 May 1825 and it was to open in two stages: from Cromford Wharf to Hurdlow on 29 May 1830 and from Hurdlow to Whaley Bridge on 6 July 1831. The line's total length was 33 miles and there were eight inclines worked by stationary engines along its route. Until 1833, when the first steam engines appeared, normal traction over the remainder of the route was supplied by horse.

The C&HPR was destined to remain an isolated line until a link was opened at Cromford with the Manchester, Buxton, Matlock & Midlands Junction Railway, in 1853. This was followed on 17 August 1857 with a link at Whaley Bridge with the Stockport, Disley & Whaley Bridge Railway (a line taken over by the LNWR in 1866). In 1862 the C&HPR was leased to the LNWR; it was formally absorbed by the larger company on 1 July 1887. By that date certain work had been undertaken to eliminate some of the inherited inclines — a deviation allowed the closure of Hurdlow incline in 1869 and Hopton incline was eased in 1877 to allow for locomotive haulage.

The absorption of the C&HPR by the LNWR allowed for the route to be rebuilt at its northern end and its incorporation within the rest of the LNWR network in the area. The result was the closure of the Ladmanlow-Shallcross section (with two inclines) on 25 June 1892.

The line, along with the rest of the LNWR, passed to the LMS in 1923. After Nationalisation the remaining sections of the line gradually disappeared, although as late as 1965 new electric winding motors could be installed at Sheep Pasture incline; they had a life of barely two years! The first post Nationalisation casualty was the stump at Whaley Bridge (separated from the rest of the line since 1892) which closed on 9 April 1952. This was followed on 2 August 1954 by the section from Old Harpur to Ladmanlow. The rest of the line survived until the early 1960s, but then closure came quickly. The section from Friden to Steeplehouse (including the Middleton incline) succumbed on 12 August 1963. That was followed on 9 April 1967 by the line between Steeplehouse, via Sheep Pasture incline, to Cromford; this closure was marked by the running of a number of enthusiasts' specials. Six months later, on 2 October 1967, the line between Parsley Hay and Friden closed as did that between Parsley Hay and Hindlow on 21 November the same year. The final section of the old C&HPR, between Hindlow and Harpur Hill, disappeared on 19 December 1973.

However, this was not quite to be the end of the C&HPR as, even before the final closure in 1973, the decision had been made to convert the line into a long-distance footpath, whilst a number of the stationary engine houses also remain to remind visitors of one of the most interesting of Britain's pioneering railways.

Sheep Pasture

Then: Undated

The Cromford & High Peak Railway is possibly one of the most interesting railways covered in this book and three comparison shots can hardly do it justice. It has, however, been covered in detail in other publications. Sheep Pasture incline formed part of the first section of the line to open on 29 May 1830. The gradient up the incline was 1 in 8 and the catchpit can just be seen where the lines divide. The remains of a wagon which ran away in 1965 can apparently still be seen today in the pit.

Middleton Top

Then: Undated

Like Sheep Pasture, the incline to Middleton Top also formed part of the original C&HPR which opened on 29 May 1830. The gradient at this point was 1 in 8.25.

Hopton Incline

Then: Circa 1930s

Locomotive operation over the incline — which had gradients of 1 in 60 (200yd), 1 in 30 (75yd), 1 in 20 (100yd), 1 in 14 (200yd) and then 1 in 470 to the top — started in April 1877. The ex-North London Railway tank locomotives arrived during the 1930s. Ten of them being transferred to work the line. The local restriction for these locomotives was five loaded and seven unloaded wagons up the incline. Often the trains were double-headed. No 27521 derailed with fatal consequences on 6 October 1937 when charging the bank at possibly 60mph — an incredible speed for these little engines. A restriction of 40mph was then imposed. Ex-WD 0-6-0STs replaced the ex-NLR locomotives in April 1956. The last service, operated by two of these replacement locomotives, Nos 68006 and 68012, was a special organised by the Stephenson Locomotive Society. It managed to stall near the top of the bank and had to reverse before being split.

Now: 11 January 1995
Although the line has closed and there
remains no trace of the engine which worked
the incline other than the flue from the
boilers, the engine house is intact as an
empty shell. At the bottom of the incline a
small museum has been developed to explain
to tourists the wonders of the line.
Ian Allan Library/Author

Now: 11 January 1995
The Middleton incline closed on 12 August
1963. Following closure the stationary
engine was restored by the Derbyshire
Industrial Archaeological Society, although
it is now under the control of Derbyshire
County Council. Whilst not all the engine
parts are original, many having been
replacing during its working life, it is still
operable today by the use of compressed air
and it works frequently at weekends.
Comparison between the pictures shows
what an excellent preservation project has
been achieved. The engine house has
deservedly become a popular tourist
attraction in the area.
Ian Allan Library/Author

Now: 11 January 1995
Following closure, the C&HPR was
converted for use as a long-distance
footpath. A couple of hardy walkers are seen
walking down the gradient in early January
1995. On the left, behind the mound, is a
factory.
H. C. Casserley/Author

Midland Railway

The Midland Railway, established by the 'Railway King' George Hudson, was the first of the major Victorian railway companies to emerge. Formed by an Act of Parliament in 1844, the MR represented the union of a number of regional companies in the North Midlands: the Midland Counties (from Derby to Nottingham, Leicester and Rugby — opened in stages during 1839 and 1840); the North Midland (from Derby to Leeds — opened 30 June 1840); and, the Birmingham & Derby — opened on 5 August 1839). Before Hudson's disgrace in 1849 the MR had expanded through the take-over of the Leicester & Swannington (the first section of which dated from 1832), the Birmingham & Gloucester (of 1840) and the Bristol & Gloucester (of 1844). It is interesting to note that the last named was constructed to broad gauge and was converted to standard gauge on the Midland's take-over.

After Hudson's fall from favour the Midland continued its expansion. For example, it took over the Leeds & Bradford Railway (which had been opened between the two towns in 1846, from Keighley to Shipley in 1847 and thence to Colne in 1848) in 1851. The line's expansion continued to be rapid. On 7 May 1857 the Leicester-Hitchin line was opened; this gave access, via the Great Northern Railway, to London. A decade later the railway constructed its own independent route south into the Metropolis, with the completion of the line from Bedford to St Pancras and, with the superb station and hotel, firmly announced its presence. A further decade on, in 1876, and after a dispute with the London & North Western Railway, the Midland completed its independent route to Scotland — the famed Settle-Carlisle line — which was probably the last major route to be constructed in the traditional method by an army of navvies.

By the turn of the century, the Midland, through a combination of take-overs and new works, had built a railway that had its tentacles stretching far and wide over the realm. It was a major player in many of the most famous of the joint railways — such as the Cheshire Lines Committee (which it joined in 1865), the Somerset & Dorset and the Midland & Great Northern — and during the last 30 years of the 19th century had taken over a number of other lines — such as the Wolverhampton & Walsall (1876), the Bedford &

St Pancras

Then: June 1951

The Midland Railway's London traffic was routed via Hitchin and the Great Northern Railway from 1857, but the traffic arrangements were never wholly satisfactory and, as a result, a line was promoted southwards from Bedford in the early 1860s. St Pancras station opened on 1 October 1868. It provided London with another superb station, the combination of Gilbert Scott's Gothic hotel and the remarkable train shed designed by Barlow. This official photograph has caught to perfection the station throat as a Midland '4F' pulls away from the famous station at 10.45am with a special boat train to Tilbury.

Now: February 1995

Electrification prevents the photographer getting exactly the same elevation as a Sheffield-bound InterCity 125, with power car No 43058 leading, departs from the station. Barlow's magnificent train shed survives, whilst the hotel, after a period of neglect, is now being restored. A number of new structures are apparent on the right. The four sidings on the left, the signalbox and the semaphore signals have long since gone. If current proposals to use St Pancras as the terminus of the Channel rail link come to fruition then this view will change completely.

Ian Allan Library/Brian Morrison

Northampton (1885) and the Kettering, Thrapston & Huntingdon (1897). Its expansionist policy reached its ultimate in 1912 when it took over the London, Tilbury & Southend.

Initially, at least, the Grouping in 1923 looked like a triumph for Derby over Euston. The locomotives and rolling stock emerged in liveries that were remarkably akin to those of the former Midland Railway, and many of the senior positions were filled by men heavily influenced by the traditions of Derby. In particular, locomotive development, at least initially, saw a perpetuation of Midland policies. This was no doubt aided by the fact that the Chief Mechanical Engineer of the LMS between 1925 and 1931 was Sir Henry Fowler, who had been CME to the Midland between 1909 and 1923.

In many respects, however, Euston was to have the last laugh, since much of the investment into the ex-LMR lines since 1948 has gone to the ex-LNWR routes. The ex-Midland main line north from St Pancras to Derby, Nottingham, Sheffield and Leeds has been very much the Cinderella of the three surviving London-north of England main lines. The Settle-Carlisle route, although long threatened with closure has managed to survive; indeed with the reopening of local stations can now look to the future with greater optimism than for many years. Other ex-Midland lines, however, have been less fortunate. Whole stretches of ex-MR metals have disappeared completely. The old main line from Matlock to Manchester was closed in 1968 (although it is now being slowly restored by preservationists).

Other ex-Midland lines that are now just a memory include Ashchurch-Great Malvern and Ashschurch-Redditch, Northampton-Bedford, Bedford-Hitchin, Three Cocks Junction-Hereford, Leicester-Market Harborough, many of the lines in the Derby and Nottingham area, and the line from Wennington to Morecambe (over part of which the Midland operated its pioneering electric services from 1908). There are, moreover, encouraging signs of a revival for certain routes. Apart from the Matlock-Buxton line currently being restored by Peak Rail, the line north from Nottingham through Mansfield to Worksop — the so-called Robin Hood Line — is being restored for a new passenger service. North of Leeds, the ex-Leeds & Bradford lines serving Bradford Forster Square and Skipton, which were once threatened with closure, are currently being electrified, as is the branch to Ilkley.

Certain sections of the Midland have also survived into preservation. Of these, the most famous is, perhaps, the Keighley & Worth Valley Light Railway. This short branch line has now been operated by the preservation society for longer than it was owned either by BR or the LMS. With its stone-built stations and traditional Midland-pattern signalboxes it is the almost perfect epitome of the old Midland Railway. A similar feel can also be obtained from the Midland Railway Project at Butterley, a site that is appropriately close to the old Midland Railway heart at Derby.

Silkstream Junction, Hendon

Then: 25 May 1957
A Stanier 2-6-4T No 42595 gives off a good exhaust as it heads north on a St Pancras-St Albans local service.
Now: 18 February 1995
Electrification work started on the line from St Pancras to Bedford in the late 1970s but, as a result of an industrial dispute over the manning of the new trains, electric services were not introduced until 1983. The pattern of services was altered by the completion of the Thameslink project and one of the Class 319 EMUs built for the Thameslink services, No 319042, forms the 14.31 service from Farringdon to St Albans.
Brian Morrison (2)

Mill Hill Broadway

Then: 8 August 1959
One of the large-boilered Stanier 2-6-2Ts, No 40142 of Kentish Town shed, departs from the station with a down service.
Now: 18 February 1995
This is a fascinating comparison and shows how the completion of the M1 motorway into London has completely changed the scene. Although the Midland line is now electrified, the actual layout remains largely unchanged; the 9³/₄ mile post still stands helping to identify precisely the position. However, the houses in the background now have the motorway separating them from the railway. Class 319/1 No 319170 forms the 14.00 Thameslink service from Gatwick Airport to Luton.
A. Swain/Brian Morrison

Elstree Tunnel

Then: 21 March 1953
The tunnel at Elstree was one of a number of major engineering works that the Midland had to complete as part of its London extension. The Midland main line was originally only double track, but the section north to Elstree was quadrupled in the 1890s and later this was extended further north. This required the completion of a second tunnel at Elstree. Here the down 'Thames-Clyde' express makes an impressive exit from the tunnel headed by Holbeck-based 'Jubilee' No 45675 *Hardy*. The locomotive remained based in Leeds until withdrawal in 1967.

Mill Hill Broadway (north)

Then: 25 May 1957
Pictured between Mill Hill Broadway and
Elstree & Borehamwood stations,
immaculate BR Standard Class 4MT
No 75041 makes a fine sight as it heads a
semi-fast down service from St Pancras to
Bedford.

Now: 18 February 1995
Trees growing on the embankment prevent
an identical shot being taken, but the 15.31
Thameslink service from Farringdon to St
Albans is captured heading northwards. The
bridge, along with many others on the route,
was rebuilt to facilitate the 25kV
electrification. From behind the wall on the
left comes the incessant noise of the M1.
Brian Morrison (2)

Now: 20 February 1995
Although suburban services are now
electrified, long distance trains over the
Midland main line are diesel-powered in the
form of InterCity 125s. These, however, do
not make such an impression when leaving
tunnels! Unit No 43045 *The Grammar
School, Doncaster, AD1350* heads the 13.00
St Pancras-Nottingham service. Apart from
the electrification and the growth of the
bushes, little has changed over the years.
Brian Morrison (2)

Elstree & Borehamwood

Then: 25 May 1957
A heavy 15-coach express from Nottingham to St Pancras, powered by Stanier Class 5 No 45335 and elderly Midland '2P' No 40485, makes a fine sight as it heads past the station.
Now: 20 February 1995
At the same location lineside growth now partly blots out the view of Class 319/0 Thameslink EMU No 319054 as it forms the 12.10 service from Bedford to Brighton.
Brian Morrison (2)

St Albans

Then: Circa 1950
The first railways to reach St Albans was the LNWR branch to Abbey which opened in 1848. This was followed by the Great Northern branch in 1865 and it was not until the opening of the Midland's London extension in 1868 that the city was placed on a main line. The up 9am Manchester-St Pancras express headed by 'Jubilee' No 45616 *Malta GC* passes the locomotive shed. The depot opened in 1868 as a small two-road building.
Now: 12 February 1995
The shed officially closed on 11 January 1960, but it was still standing as late as July 1967. Also vanished are the semaphore signals and the track nearest to the camera in the 'Then' shot. The listed signalbox, however, remains to provide a reference as the 08.39 Sheffield-St Pancras InterCity 125, headed by Class 43 No 43061 *City of Lincoln* passes through.
E. D. Bruton/Brian Morrison

Bedford (Midland Road)

Then: January 1962

Although the Midland's extension south from Leicester was first promoted in the 1840s, it fell a victim of the collapse of many schemes in the 'Railway Mania' and the demise of the 'Railway King', George Hudson. The Act allowing construction of the line from Leicester to Hitchin was passed in 1853 and it was opened throughout on 8 May 1857. The use of GNR metals from Hitchin to provide access to London was not wholly successful and pressure grew for the building of an independent line from Bedford southwards. The construction of the Midland main line relegated the Hitchin branch to secondary status. Ex-LMS Class 2MT 2-6-2T No 41225 waits at the station with the push-pull service to Hitchin.

Now: 12 February 1995

The Hitchin branch lost its passenger services on 1 January 1962 and the final section to close completely, that between Bedford and Cardington, succumbed in April 1969. The platform building seen behind the locomotive in the 'Then' shot and the right-hand platform have both been demolished. A Thameslink Class 319 EMU No 319173 awaits departure with a service to Brighton.

J. C. Baker/Ian Allan Library

Bedford (Midland Road) (north)

Then June 1960
A dirty-looking Midland Class 4F No 44381 heads an up freight heading for Sandy. From Bedford this train would have been routed over the ex-LNWR route towards Cambridge.

Now: 12 February 1995
The tracks to the right of the 'Then' photograph, including the line on which the '4F' was running would have been to the right of the fence. They were, however, removed following the closure of the line links to the East Coast main line. Bedford station has been subsequently rebuilt and the tracks realigned. The main lines to the left and the road bridge are all that remain to identify precisely the location. The Thameslink units visible are stabled.

J. C. Baker/Brian Morrison

Bedford Goods/
Ouse Bridge Junction

Then: 1 June 1963
Fairburn 2-6-4T No 42174 is shown leaving
this once busy yard with a freight train
destined for the Hitchin branch.
Now: 12 February 1995
Today things are much quieter. The newly-
constructed carriage sidings do not show any
activity. Being a Sunday, the Bedford-
Bletchley trains were not running. The goods
yard and road bridge in the distance provide
reference points, but the signalbox has
disappeared.
A. W. Smith/Brian Morrison

Oakley

Then: 9 April 1964
This station, which closed on 15 September
1958 to passenger services and to freight in
August 1963, was situated just a short
distance north of Bedford on the Midland
main line and was located at the top of the
short gradient encountered before the water
troughs and Sharnbrook Bank. Class 5 No
45289 heads a rake of tube stock northwards
passed the remains of the station.
Now: 12 February 1995
Class 60 No 60098 *Charles Francis Brush*
passes the station site hauling a rake of
'Mainline Freight' ballast hoppers
southbound. Although all traces of the
station have gone, the houses and trees
remain in the background.
A. Davenport/Brian Morrison

Olney

Then: 8 February 1958
Olney was one of three intermediate stations on the Midland branch from Bedford to Northampton. The line opened on 10 June 1872 and was worked from the outset by the MR, although it was not actually owned by the company until 1885. Stanier 2-6-2T No 40182 is pictured calling at the station with the 3.8pm service from Northampton.

Wellingborough

Then: 19 April 1963
The station at Wellingborough dates from 1857. It was an important junction station on the Midland main line from Kettering to Bedford, particularly for freight. A Class 4F 0-6-0 is caught crossing from the down slow line to the yards north of the station.

Wellingborough (north)

Then: 26 August 1953
It was in 1867 that tenders were accepted for the building of a roundhouse, although locomotive servicing facilities existed before that date. In the busy scene, dominated by No 2 shed, Compound No 41079 approaches the station on an up local train as Stanier Class 8F No 48350 also heads south on an up coal train.

Now: 16 February 1995
Passenger services over the line were withdrawn on 5 March 1962, although freight continued until January 1964. The line continued in use to serve a military depot at Piddington from Northampton until 1981. There was also single-road shed at Olney for the Towcester service, but this closed in 1928. I needed the help of a local resident to identify the location; the house is virtually on the station site.
T. Roundthwaite/Author

Now: 16 February 1995
The station building remains intact, but there has been a considerable rationalisation in the track layout. Gone is the link to the now-closed ex-LNWR line from Northampton to Peterborough (which was located just to the south of the station). Passenger services are now formed of frequent InterCity 125 units to and from St Pancras, whilst there also remains limited freight and parcels traffic through the station. The 14.30 St Pancras-Sheffield service, formed of power cars Nos 43052 and 43053, rushes past the station non-stop.
C. P. Boocock/Author

Now: 16 February 1995
The No 1 shed was demolished in July 1964, before the shed closed to steam operation on 13 June 1966. After that date the shed continued to service diesels, but that has now finished. The No 2 shed remains standing and is currently available for industrial use. The water tower is also still extant; this was located outside the No 1 shed. Between the two sheds was the stabling point for the ex-LMS Garretts. Against a background of unused sidings, the 14.38 Nottingham-St Pancras service heads south powered by InterCity 125 units Nos 43059 and 43066.
T. B. Paisley/Author

Kettering

Then: 24 April 1957
The Midland Railway route from Leicester to Hitchin opened to passenger services on 8 May 1857 and Kettering station dates from the building of the line.

Now: 16 February 1995
It is remarkable how little has changed at this station over the past 38 years. Whilst there has been the inevitable rationalisation of track, along with the loss of signalboxes and locomotive shed, the actual station building retains many of the superb features that it gained when built. Although reroofed, the platform canopies — which elsewhere have been easy victims of modernisation — remain along with the decorative ironwork of the supports. An InterCity 125, formed of power cars Nos 43072 and 43055, is arriving on the 13.39 service from Nottingham to St Pancras.
Ian Allan Library/Author

Market Harborough

Then: 19 September 1964
Although it was the LNWR that was the first railway to reach Market Harborough (in 1850), it was the opening of the Midland Railway's Leicester-Hitchin route in 1857 that put the town on main line to the south. Here a special sponsored by the Locomotive Club of Great Britain headed by rebuilt 'Royal Scot' No 46155 *The Lancers* makes a fine sight as it heads north past No 3 signalbox. The lines on the extreme right, which can be seen curving behind the signalbox are the ex-LNWR lines to Northampton; these used to run north of Market Harborough to Luffenham and Peterborough.

Now: 16 February 1995
Very little remains today to identify the location, except the bridge abutment on the left. It was not possible to get the same elevation as before to illustrate InterCity 125 No 43049 *Neville Hill* working the 12.30 St Pancras-Sheffield service. The ex-LNWR line to Northampton was closed completely on 31 May 1980, although there are plans to reopen part of it as a preserved line.
G. D. King/Author

Leicester station

Then: 12 April 1958
The Midland Counties line from Trent to Leicester opened on 5 May 1840 and from Leicester to Rugby later the same year. However, Leicester (London Road) station was rebuilt in 1892. Here we are looking to the south. Fowler 2-6-4T No 42339 is ready to leave with the 11am service to Nottingham, whilst Ivatt 2-6-2T No 41268 is undertaking station pilot duties. This was the last day of steam working on these Leicester-Nottingham services.

Now: 23 January 1995
Although the main station buildings remain, there is evidence of rebuilding at platform level. The siding area to the west of the station has been converted into a car park.
A. F. Taylor/Author

Leicester (north)

Then: 16 August 1980
The 'Leicester Gap' represented one of the last stretches of semaphore signalling on the ex-Midland main line and it was not until the early 1980s that significant changes were made. Prior to the elimination of manual signalling, two Class 31s, Nos 31313 and 31176, approach the station with the Saturdays Only 09.50 Norwich-Birmingham service.

Now: 23 January 1995
With the conversion to MAS, the track was rationalised as can be seen from this photograph of a Derby Research Centre unit heading south. The wider angle allows for the inclusion of the diesel stabling point on the extreme right, where Class 56 No 56103 and Class 58 No 58050 can be seen.

Author (2)

Woodville

Then: Undated
This station was situated to the east of Burton upon Trent on a loop line which went through to Moira on the main Burton-Leicester line. Midland '4F' No 43836 pilots 'Crab' 2-6-0 No 42765 past the station with a returning special from Blackpool to the Midlands. The photograph post dates the closure of the station to passenger traffic, as passenger services were withdrawn on 6 October 1947.

Now: 4 February 1995
The station closed completely in 1964 and little now remains to remind the reader that a railway once passed this site. It was not possible to get exactly the same angle, but all signs of the impressive Mansfield Brothers tile and sanitary ware factory have completely disappeared. The platform for the station can just be found in the undergrowth. The 'Crab' does, however, survive and can now be found restored on the East Lancs Railway.
Ian Allan Library/Author

Syston

Then: 27 July 1963
This was the point where the Midland main line divided, with lines heading south to Leicester, east to Melton Mowbray and north to Nottingham. This fine shot shows a Stanier Class 5, No 44869, at the head of the 8.30pm Leicester-Scarborough service. The station at Syston can be seen in the distance.

Now: 23 January 1995
The triangular junction at Syston remains in use, although the original station closed here in March 1968 (it has recently reopened). As can be seen, the track layout has been drastically reduced as Sprinter No 156417 approaches the new platform, which is visible on the photographer's side of the road overbridge.
G. D. King/Author

Trent

Then: 3 July 1956
Situated to the west of Nottingham, Trent was an important junction. Lines radiated from this point to Nottingham, Chesterfield, Derby and Leicester. Ex-Midland Compound No 41095 makes a leaky departure from the station with the 8.7am Derby-Nottingham train. The down north curve line can be seen branching away to the right.

Now: 2 January 1995
Although the network of lines in the area remains largely intact, albeit rationalised, the station itself closed on 1 January 1968. It was only due to the help of a local railwayman that I knew where to stand to get the comparison shot. The marker point was the bridge abutment deep in the undergrowth. Pacer Unit No 150104, painted in Centro livery, passes the once busy and complex station site.
A. W. Smith/Author

Beeston

Then: Early 1950s

The station is situated to the west of Nottingham on the line towards Trent. It was one of three intermediate stations opened when the Midland Counties Railway introduced passenger services on the line between Derby and Nottingham on 30 May 1839. Here Midland Compound No 41084, with 'British Railways' lettering on the tender, arrives at the station with a stopping train for Derby.

Now: 21 January 1995

The station remains open and the main difference, apart from the loss of the Midland Railway signalbox, is that the level crossing featured in the 'Then' photograph has been replaced by a road overbridge. The goods yard is now occupied by a Blue Circle Cement site, which is rail connected. Class 158 No 158780 is leaving the station with a service for Lincoln.

C. T. Goode/Author

Trowell

Then: 9 July 1966
This station was on the Midland main line north from Trent towards Chesterfield. Holbeck-based 'Jubilee' No 45562 *Alberta* is passing through the station working the summer Saturdays Only service from Poole to Bradford. The locomotive had taken over the service at Nottingham.

Basford

Then: 27 July 1963
'Crab' 2-6-0 No 42855 passes the signalbox at Basford, on the Nottingham-Worksop line, at the head of the Saturdays Only 11.24am service from Mablethorpe to Radford via Mansfield.

Nottingham (west)

Then: 9 July 1966
Although the coaling stage at the shed was still standing when this photograph of 'Jubilee' No 45562 *Alberta* was taken, the shed itself had been closed for 15 months by this date. The locomotive was at the head of the summer Saturdays Only service from Bradford to Poole, which had travelled via Huddersfield, Penistone and Sheffield. A 'Peak' diesel-electric would replace the steam locomotive at Nottingham, and the 'Jubilee' would then head to Colwick shed for servicing.

Now: 3 January 1995
Trowell station closed on 2 January 1967 and apart from the enlarged bridge abutments in the distance, nothing remains to indicate that there was once a station at this site. The lines towards Nottingham can be seen sweeping away to the left through the bridge, whilst those on the right head towards Toton. Class 158 No 158780 is passing the site of the old station with the 10.51 Liverpool-Norwich service.
G. L. Allen/Author

Now: 21 January 1995
Although passenger services over the line were withdrawn on 12 October 1964, the bulk of the route survived to serve many of the collieries that once abounded in this part of Nottinghamshire. Now rechristened the 'Robin Hood' line, passenger services are being gradually restored north from Radford to Mansfield and Worksop. The first stage opened in 1993 through Basford and the line currently terminates at Newstead, 10.25 miles from Nottingham. Sprinter No 156403 is caught on the 12.02 service from Newstead. The signalbox has long gone and the sidings are lifted, being replaced by an industrial estate.
T. G. Hepburn/Author

Now: 2 January 1995
The extensive yards at this point have gone and the land has been redeveloped for industrial use. Sprinter No 156415 passes with the 11.18 service from Crewe, which will eventually work to Skegness.
J. Cupit/Author

Nottingham (Midland)

Then: 7 August 1956
The railway reached Nottingham, courtesy of the Midland Counties Railway, in 1839, although the station that stands today owes more to the reconstruction that was completed in 1904 and designed by A. E. Lambert. The impressive station buildings are visible in the background as one of the Holbeck-based Class 5s fitted with double chimney and Caprotti valve gear approaches the station and an '8F' trundles westwards.

Now: 2 January 1995
The area approaching the station has changed out of all recognition with the goods yard being replaced by an impressive new Magistrates' Court complex currently under construction. The super station building, however, remains. A Class 156 Sprinter No 156422 heads away from the station with the 10.36 Skegness-Crewe train.

J. P. Wilson/Author

Rolleston Junction

Then: 12 June 1959

This junction, situated just to the west of Newark, was the point where the Midland branch serving Southwell diverged from the main line linking Nottingham and Lincoln. Here one of the ex-Midland 0-4-4Ts, No 58065, is ready to depart with the 6.55pm service to Southwell. These trains were amongst the last workings for this type of engine and passenger services over the branch were withdrawn three days after the date of this photograph. Freight services to Southwell continued until withdrawal in December 1964.

Now: 23 January 1995

Although no longer a junction, Rolleston continues to be served by passenger trains on the Nottingham-Lincoln route. However, as can be seen, the station buildings that were situated on this platform have been demolished; the angle of photography is slightly different as the location of the 'Then' photograph was covered by dense undergrowth. The Newark-Nottingham line can be seen on the extreme left.

F. A. Quayle/Author

Peterborough

Then: 6 June 1960
The Midland Railway reached Peterborough in 1848 with the completion of the line from Leicester via Manton Junction. Midland services to Peterborough were always overshadowed by those of the Great Northern. Despite this the Midland possessed a shed in the town, built in 1872 and known as Spittal Bridge. In 1933 the shed had an allocation of 46. Class 4F 0-6-0 No 44521 is caught leaving Peterborough with a train to Leicester via Stamford.

Now: 14 January 1995
Peterborough remains an important junction on the now-electrified East Coast main line and services continue to operate over the ex-Midland line through Stamford. Today Class 158s operate a frequent cross-country service from Norwich or Cambridge to Birmingham, Liverpool or other destinations. Unit No 158844 is leaving on the 13.00 Norwich-Liverpool (Line Street) train. In the background can be seen Class 58 No 58032 and various Class 31s at the stabling point. The station layout was considerably modernised to provide two fast through lines and the station building itself has been rebuilt.

M. Mensing/Author

Stamford (Town)

Then: 22 June 1960
The impressive station building at Stamford was built for the opening of the line in 1848 and was probably designed by Sancton Wood. It is one of the most important intermediate stations on the Leicester-Peterborough line. Rugby-allocated Fairburn 2-6-4T No 42061 is arriving with a Leicester (London Road)-Peterborough (East) train.

Now: 22 January 1995
There have been remarkably few changes to the station building, although the platform signage has moved with the times. The area of the goods shed is being redeveloped and the station now houses one of the country's leading dealers in secondhand railway publications. Heading west, Class 158 No 158862 calls at the station with the 13.55 from Cambridge to Birmingham.

Manton Junction

Then: 23 June 1956
Manton is the point where the Midland line to Peterborough diverged from the line south through Corby to Kettering. The line from Leicester to Peterborough opened in 1848 and that south from Manton to Kettering saw local passenger services introduced on 1 November 1880. A Stanier '8F' No 48507 takes the line towards Peterborough with a freight. It is approaching the station at Manton, the platform of which can be seen on the extreme right.

Oakham

Then: 6 August 1960
Like Stamford, Oakham was built for the opening of the line from Leicester to Peterborough in 1848 and was also probably the work of Sancton Wood. Ivatt 2-6-0 No 43081 is calling at the station with a local stopping train for Peterborough.
Now: 23 January 1995
Oakham station remains open, the only station in Rutland (England's smallest county) to survive. Not a great deal has changed over the past 35 years as the diverted 08.39 InterCity 125 from Sheffield to St Pancras passes through headed by No 43156.
P. H. Wells/Author

Wigston South Junction

Then: 22 August 1959
Stanier '8F' No 48319 approaches Wigston Magna with an up coal train. This complex junction of lines, which effectively formed part of a triangle with the ex-LNWR line towards Nuneaton and the ex-Midland line towards Rugby, is situated just south of Leicester.
Now: 23 January 1995
Passenger and freight services over the line to Rugby were withdrawn on 1 January 1962 and there has been a great deal of rationalisation over the years. An InterCity 125 rushes past at around 80mph on the 14.24 service from Sheffield to St Pancras.
M. Mensing/Author

Now: 22 January 1995
The line south through Corby used to be very busy, but it has now been singled. Passenger services over the route were withdrawn on 6 June 1966 and the line retained for use by freight and trains diverted as a result of engineering work from the Midland main line. The diversions represent, along with railtours, the only opportunities to cross the Welland Valley over the spectacular Harringworth Viaduct that is 1,275yd long. Passenger services, however, continue to use the Leicester-Peterborough line and Class 158 No 158797 rushes by on the 12.17 Birmingham-Cambridge service. *J. F. Oxley/Author*

Bennerley

Then: 14 September 1954
'Jubilee' No 45636 *Uganda* heads south along the ex-Midland main line at Bennerley with a Bradford-St Pancras express via Trent and Leicester. In the background can be seen the viaduct which carried the ex-Great Northern Railway line from Nottingham to Derby across the Midland lines.
Now: 3 January 1995
The viaduct remains, although the ex-GNR line is now closed. It is a listed structure and work was underway to repair it when this photograph was taken. Class 60 No 60017 *Arenig Fawr* heads an up merry-go-round train towards Toton. In line with the decline of coal traffic nationwide, the number of mgr trains over this line has been significantly reduced over recent years.
J. P. Wilson/Author

Derby (south)

Then: 25 May 1959
Fowler 2-6-4T No 42140 leaves with the 5.8pm local train to Nottingham whilst Ivatt 2-6-0 No 46497 busies itself with station pilot duties. Part of the works complex can be seen in the right background, along with the footbridge across all the lines above the station; this used to provide an excellent vantage point for photography.

Now: 2 January 1995
Sadly the south end view, which until recently was uncluttered, has been ruined with the gantry and portable buildings. Sprinter No 156418 leaves on the 13.16 service from Crewe to Nottingham. The railways first reached Derby in 1839; it was to achieve fame as the home of the Midland Railway but almost 150 years on much of the old works has closed, although part of the site is being taken over by Waterman Railways as its base.
R. C. Riley/Author

Wirksworth

Then: 5 August 1952
The branch to Wirksworth opened on 1 October 1867. This is a view from the overbridge looking towards Duffield, where the line joined the Midland main line north of Derby, and '4F' No 44164 can be seen on the line to the quarry sidings. By this date passenger services, which had been withdrawn on 16 June 1947, had ceased.

Now: 2 January 1995
Although general freight traffic over the branch was withdrawn in 1968, the line remained open for quarry trains until the early 1990s. Subsequently a number of passenger specials have operated over the line. The track remains intact and there is talk of a preservation scheme should traffic from the quarry not resume.
R. H. Hughes/Author

Ambergate

Then: 12 May 1967
The original station at Ambergate was replaced by the famous triangular station in 1876. Here we see a freight train headed by an unidentified Stanier Class 8F running up the Derwent Valley towards Matlock. The train has come from the Codnor Park line and is caught passing the West Junction box.

Now: 2 January 1995
The facilities at Ambergate have been much reduced; the lines from North to West junctions and Station to North junctions were closed on 26 February 1967, and the main line between Derby and Manchester was severed north of Matlock in 1968. The station at Ambergate is now represented by this single platform on the branch to Matlock. Class 150/1 Sprinter No 150129 is leaving on the 15.03 service from Derby. The whole area is now very enclosed by trees.
J. P. Wilson/Author

Cromford

Then: Undated
This ornate station, situated on the Midland main line from Ambergate towards Manchester (opened between Ambergate and Rowsley in 1849), dates from about 1860.
Now: 11 January 1995
Following the closure of the line north from Matlock, the line has been singled although passenger services still operate. Sprinter No 156405 calls at the station with the 11.01 service from Derby to Matlock. The station building remains, but is boarded up.
Ian Allan Library/Author

Matlock Bath

Then: Undated
Although the line between Ambergate and Rowsley opened in 1849, the station at Matlock Bath was not built until the 1880s, when Matlock was becoming popular as a health resort. The Swiss-style of architecture was designed to complement the almost Alpine landscape of the Derwent valley at this point and the Midland Railway used the location heavily in its publicity as the Switzerland of England. Stanier 'Jubilee' No 45592 *Indore* passes through the station at the head of a Manchester (Central)-St Pancras express.
Now: 11 January 1995
The station remains open to serve the Derby-Matlock local service. Class 156 No 156405 departs from the station on the 11.48 departure from Matlock to Derby. In the background can be seen High Tor through which the line passes in a tunnel before reaching the present terminus at Matlock.
J. Cupit/Author

Darley Dale
Then: Undated
This was the first station north of Matlock on the ex-Midland main line to Manchester. The busy scene, probably taken in the late 1950s, shows Fairburn 2-6-4T No 42228 leaving for Derby with a local train as 'Jubilee' No 45652 *Hawke* arrives with a down express.
Now: 11 January 1995
The station closed to passenger services on 6 March 1967 and the line itself lost its passenger trains on 1 July 1968; freight services were also withdrawn at that date. Following the lifting of the track that seemed to be the end of the story, but in the mid-1970s the Peak Railway Society was established with the ambitious aim of rebuilding the Matlock-Buxton route as a preserved steam railway. Darley Dale is now the main base for the group and track is now laid to Matlock in the south and progress is being made northwards. The original signalbox was demolished, but a replacement Midland-pattern box was obtained. A Class 03 shunter is parked on the down line, whilst the yard with some of the preserved stock is visible beyond the crossing.
D. Sellman/Author

Rowsley

Then: 3 July 1963

Rowsley was the terminus of the line from Ambergate from its opening until the completion of the Midland line northwards in the 1860s. The extension required a minor deviation at Rowsley with the result that a new station, designed by Edward Walters, was constructed. Rowsley was the main freight centre on the line and had a sizeable shed, which closed in 1964. Class 5 No 45071 passes the station with a northbound freight.

Now: 11 January 1995

The passenger station closed on 6 March 1967 and all passenger and freight services over the line were withdrawn on 1 July 1968. Today very little remains of the railway and the site is an industrial estate. All that could change, however, if the ambitious plans of Peak Rail come to fruition. One of the preservationist's major obstacles lies just past the station where the railway crossed over the main A6 by a now-removed road overbridge. *G. T. Robinson/Author*

Monsal Dale

The: 27 September 1958

The Midland Railway was authorised in 1860 to build a line from Rowsley to Buxton and, following construction problems, services commenced over the line in 1863. Monsal Dale was the last station heading north before Millers Dale where the ex-Midland lines diverged north towards Chinley and Manchester and south towards Buxton. A service from Derby towards Manchester is departing from the station.

Now: 11 January 1995

Monsal Dale station lost its passenger services on 10 August 1959 and the line was closed through to both passenger and freight trains on 1 July 1968. Today the trackbed is an official footpath, although the planned reinstatement of the line by the preservation group should see trains restored in due course. *J. P. Wilson/Author*

Buxton (south)

Then: 17 June 1965
Class 4F 0-6-0 No 43967 leaves Buxton on the ex-Midland line towards Miller's Dale. On the horizon can be seen the locomotive shed, which opened in 1892, although there had been a smaller shed close to the LNWR station prior to that date. Buxton was an important railway centre, with lines linking the town with Stockport, Derby and Ashbourne.
Now: 11 January 1995
Although there has been the inevitable rationalisation of services. Buxton remains an important centre. Passenger services are now limited to the ex-LNWR line towards Stockport, but freight (predominantly limestone) continues over part of the old route to Ashbourne and over the ex-Midland line towards Peak Forest. The steam shed closed in 1968. The line to Peak Forest is now singled.
D. Cross/Author

Peak Forest

Then: 12 May 1967
A Stanier '8F', No 48442, passes the quarry at Peak Forest with an up freight. The limestone traffic from the numerous quarries around Buxton was one of the railway's most profitable freight flows.

Now: 2 February 1995
The location is not as busy as it used to be, but there is still a considerable amount of traffic out of the quarries. Class 60 No 60046 *William Wilberforce* leaves light engine *en route* for Earls Sidings. The track looks waterlogged after a period of heavy rain. In the background many of the buildings in and around the quarry have disappeared. Peak Forest station, which was on the other side of the bridge from which the photograph was taken, was closed on 6 March 1967 but remains extant as the train crew office for the area.
D. Cross/Author

Chinley East Junction

Then: 22 August 1964

This was the point where the Midland's Hope Valley line across to Sheffield met the Manchester-Buxton/Derby line. It became a junction on 1 June 1894 with the official opening of the Hope Valley route. Thompson 'B1' class 4-6-0 No 61315 still has another three miles of climbing to do before it reaches the summit of the Hope Valley line at Cowburn Tunnel. It is working the 11.30am Llandudno-Sheffield (Midland) service.

Now: 2 February 1995

The line linking the Hope Valley route to that through to Peak Forest has been singled. Passenger services over the ex-Midland branch to Buxton from Millers Dale were withdrawn on 6 March 1967, whilst passenger services through Peak Forest to Chinley lasted until 1 July 1968. Stone traffic from the limestone quarries around Buxton has ensured that the line has remained open. The signalbox is also a casualty as Class 158 No 158844 passes on the 10.51 service from Liverpool to Norwich.

G. Neve/Author

Chinley North Junction

Then: 4 March 1961
Midland Class 4F No 44250 takes the line towards Peak Forest after being held at signals.
Now: 2 February 1995
Taken from a slightly higher elevation, the 'Now' photograph illustrates well the track rationalisation that has taken place at this location since the withdrawal of passenger services on the Derby line in 1968. Class 158 No 158770 forms the 12.16 Manchester (Piccadilly)-Sheffield service.
Author (2)

Chinley (east)

Then: March 1966
An unidentified Stanier '8F' pulls away from the once busy Chinley station with a heavy ballast train.
Now: 2 February 1995
Today there are only the two through running lines, the station buildings have also been rationalised and the signalbox demolished. A Class 158, No 158774, approaches the station with the 13.09 Sheffield-Manchester (Piccadilly) service.
L. A. Nixon/Author

Chinley (west)

Then: 20 April 1968
One of the many steam specials run during the last year of main line operation on BR is shown leaving the station at Chinley, with its extensive trackwork and numerous platforms, headed by Stanier Class 5s Nos 45110 and 44949. No 45110 was to be preserved and is now on display at the Severn Valley Railway.
Now: 2 February 1995
Today the railway has been reduced to the minimum, with only two through running lines and the island platform. Class 158 No 158786 passes by non-stop on the 09.58 Norwich-Liverpool train.
Author (2)

New Mills Junction

Then: Undated

Stanier Class 5 No 45035 passes the junction as it climbs towards Peak Forest with an up express from Manchester (Central) to St Pancras. At this date the train would have called at Stockport (Tiviot Dale). Originally the Midland gained access to Manchester over a joint line with the Manchester, Sheffield & Lincolnshire Railway from New Mills via Romiley. However, the company decided to build its own direct route and this was opened on 1 July 1880.

Now: 2 February 1995

New Mills remains a junction with the line to the right heading for New Mills and Romiley. Whilst that, the remains of the 1880 route, is now linked to the Stockport Edgeley-Buxton line via a chord line built at Hazel Grove. Passenger services over the 1880 route to Manchester (Central) were withdrawn on 1 July 1968, but were restored from New Mills to Hazel Grove on 11 May 1987 on the completion of the new chord. Class 158 No 158774 rushes past on the 14.16 Manchester (Piccadilly)-Sheffield service.

K. Field/Author

Romiley

Then: 31 May 1966

This junction was situated on the joint Midland/Great Central (formerly the MS&LR) line from New Mills into Manchester. It was through here that all Midland-operated trains to and from Manchester ran until the completion in 1880 of the route via Stockport. The lines on the far left connected the line with the Woodhead route over the Pennines at Hyde. 'Jubilee' class No 45581 *Bihar & Orissa* is shown taking empty stock from New Mills to Belle Vue; this will later form a train destined for the West Riding.

Now: 1 February 1995

Although two of the running lines towards Manchester have been removed, much else remains as Class 101 DMU No 101569 heads towards Manchester through pouring rain.

I. Smith/Author

Heaton Mersey

Then: Undated
Heaton Mersey was situated on the ex-Midland line from New Mills to Manchester. It was the point where a link headed southeastwards to connect with the ex-CLC line from Stockport westwards. An unidentified 2-6-4T passes the station with empty stock from Manchester (Central) destined for Cheadle Heath.
Now: 5 February 1995
The station lost its passenger services on 3 July 1961 and freight facilities were withdrawn in October 1963. The line was, however, to survive until the late 1960s. Once again, it was extremely difficult to identify the exact spot, but fortunately I happened to ask a passer-by who was able to point me to the correct location. As will be obvious, little remains today to remind readers that once expresses from Manchester (Central) used to pass by this point *en route* to Derby and London.
W. J. Shayfield/Author

Chesterfield (Midland)

Then: 27 May 1954
The railway reached Chesterfield on 11 May 1840 when the North Midland Railway's line from Derby to Rotherham was opened without ceremony. An ex-Midland Class 4F No 44066 arrives with a local service from Elmton & Cresswell whilst in the background Class 3F No 43814 replenishes its tender at the water column as it works an up freight.
Now: 16 December 1994 (above right)
Whilst it is no longer possible to travel by train to Elmton & Cresswell — the station lost its passenger services in October 1964 and the direct route from Chesterfield via Tapton Junction closed on 5 July 1954 — little has ostensibly changed over the past 40 years to the platform structures; indeed the canopies on the up side show evidence of a more recent repaint than those of 1954. Closer examination, however, reveals that the structure behind the up platform canopy has been demolished, whilst signalling and platform lighting has also been modernised. One of the frequent InterCity 125s which serve the station arrives with the 12.24 service from Sheffield to St Pancras. Power car No 43072 *Derby Etches Park* is leading. *J. P. Wilson/Author*

Clay Cross

Then: 9 June 1968
This is and always has been a popular location for
enthusiasts to observe the trains running over the
Midland main line. It was the point where trains
from Leeds to Derby diverged from the direct main
line through Alfreton and Trowell to Trent and on
to London. As a result there was always plenty of
action. The station closed on 2 January 1967 and
evidence of dereliction has already set in as
'Britannia' Pacific No 70013 *Oliver Cromwell*, on
one of its many rail tour duties in 1968, passes with
a special from Manchester to St Pancras. The train
had been routed via the Hope Valley.
Now: 3 January 1995
Although the signalbox has gone and the platforms
have been demolished, the track layout remains
remarkably unchanged as Class 158 No 158791
passes on the 13.47 Nottingham-Manchester
Piccadilly service.
J. S. Hancock/Author

Tapton Junction

Then: 15 May 1965
When the North Midland main line was originally opened in 1840 it bypassed Sheffield, heading northeastwards from Chesterfield via Barrow Hill to Rotherham and thence to Leeds. It was only on 1 February 1870 that the Midland opened its line to Sheffield, thus creating a junction at this point. Ex-WD 2-8-0 No 90529 crosses over to the up slow at the head of a lengthy rake of mineral wagons.
Now: 3 January 1995
Although regular passenger services no longer use the old main line from Tapton to Rotherham, it is still a busy freight line and it is used for diverted passenger services. The track has been simplified and the signalbox has been demolished as Class 158 No 158797 passes with the 10.51 Liverpool-Norwich working.
J. S. Hancock/Author

Staveley/Barrow Hill

Then: 15 May 1965
The station closed to passenger services on 5 July 1954, but more than a decade later both platforms and station buildings remain remarkably intact. The extensive marshalling yards can be seen in the background. The steam shed, coded 18D until transfer to the Eastern Region in 1958 when it became 41D, was situated to the top right of the photograph. Steam was ousted from the shed in October 1965. One of the Austerity 2-8-0s, No 90572 in typical external condition, passes on a down coal train.

Now: 3 January 1995
There have been dramatic changes at this point. The old station has been completely eliminated and the marshalling yards, although they survive in part, are now little used. The famous shed at Barrow Hill was converted into a diesel depot in which guise it survived until closure in February 1991, at which time it was the last traditional roundhouse to remain operational on British Rail. There are now hopes that it will be preserved as an example of a Midland roundhouse. Class 60 No 60007 *Robert Adam* passes with an empty Corby-Lackenby steel train.
J. S. Hancock/Author

Dore & Totley

Then: September 1960
The 4.30pm slow service from Chinley to Sheffield pulls into the station headed by Midland Class 4F No 44211. It was here that the Midland's Hope Valley line diverged from the main Sheffield-Chesterfield route. Just to the west of this location was the longest tunnel on the LMS — Totley — which measures three miles 950yd in length. The four platforms of the station are visible; the two furthest from the camera served the main line southwards. The Midland main line at this point opened on 1 February 1870, but it was not until 1 June 1894 that the Hope Valley route was opened to passenger services. The station at Dore & Totley opened on 1 February 1872.
Now: 16 December 1964
Today the station remains open, but only a single platform survives to serve the trains between Sheffield and Manchester over the Hope Valley route. The attractive Midland signalbox and the semaphore signals have disappeared. Class 158 No 158775 passes with the 13.09 Sheffield-Manchester (Piccadilly) service. This working originated from Cleethorpes at 11.26.
K. Smith/Author

Sheffield (Midland)

Then: 5 October 1957
Although the first section of what was later to form the Midland Railway reached Sheffield with the opening of the Sheffield & Rotherham Railway in 1838, the line that served Sheffield (Midland) was not completed until 1870 and the station itself was rebuilt to the design of Charles Trubshaw in the first decade of the 20th century. Holbeck-allocated Compound No 41068, in terrible external condition, is waiting to leave for Fleetwood with a train of empty fish wagons.
Now: 3 March 1995
Although fish traffic is now very much a thing of the past, much else at Sheffield remains unchanged. The station layout has not altered dramatically, although, as can be seen the old footbridge has gone. The entrance to the station has been modernised and the surrounding area completely redeveloped. The modern building overshadowing the station is one of BR's many 1960s office blocks.
J. F. Henton/Author

Rotherham (Masborough)

Then: 12 July 1963

Rotherham was the initial terminus of the North Midland main line from Derby until the extension to Leeds opened on 30 June 1840. This was not, however, the first railway to reach the town as the Sheffield & Rotherham Railway, another of the Midland's constituents, opened on 1 November 1838. The station was rebuilt in the 1880s. The 4.10pm Leeds (City)-Sheffield (Midland) local stopping service departs from the station behind Holbeck-based Stanier Class 5 No 44662.

Now: 3 January 1995

The ex-Midland station was closed and replaced by a new Rotherham Central station on 11 May 1987 following the completion of the Holmes Chord, which allowed trains over the Midland route to be diverted to the new, and more central, station. The new station now serves all the local trains from Sheffield to Leeds or Doncaster. The original lines, however, remain, and Class 158 No 158781 is seen passing the derelict platforms at Masborough whilst working the 13.26 service from Cleethorpes to Manchester (Piccadilly).

D. P. Leckanby/Author

Normanton

Then: 2 July 1966

Normanton was one of the earliest and most important railway junctions in the formative years of Britain's railways. It was effectively the point where the L&YR and the MR met. Originally dating back to 1850, the shed at Normanton grew considerably over the years and in the 1920s the Midland had around 60 locomotives based at the shed. The location was always interesting as it was a point where locomotives from various regions could be seen side by side. Local Stanier Class 5 No 45080 is shown heading an up freight whilst an '03' diesel shunter is visible in the background.

Now: 23 February 1995

I think that this is one of the most dramatic comparison shots in the whole book. The shed finally closed on 2 October 1967, although it remained available for servicing steam locomotives until January 1968. Gradually the goods yards fell out of use as the coal industry in the area declined along with other local industries. In complete contrast to the cluttered scene of 1966 Class 60 No 60056 *William Beveridge* passes through light engine *en route* back to Peak Forest. Although the site has been considered for a new European freight terminal, there are as yet few signs to be seen of it.

Author (2)

Stourton (Leeds)

Then: 23 March 1961/21 August 1979
Stourton is situated on the Midland main line from Wortley Junction, via Woodlesford, to Altofts and Normanton. The first of the two 'Then' photographs was taken from the steps of the signalbox and shows rebuilt 'Royal Scot' No 46118 *Royal Welch Fusilier* heading the down 'Waverley' express towards Leeds. The Midland signalbox features prominently in the second 'Then' shot, which also shows Class 31 No 31319 passing with a down freight. Behind the Class 31 is the old wagon repair works, a building which at one time was also used to store Class 20s.

Now: 14 December 1994
The route from Leeds to Altofts and Normanton has been much downgraded, particularly with the closure of the old Midland main line as a through route via Cudworth. Local services between Leeds and Wakefield (Kirkgate) and Castleford still provide a passenger service. One of the West Yorkshire PTE's Class 141s, No 141111, is passing the site of the now-demolished wagon works. The angle of the 'Now' photograph also shows the Freightliner terminal at Stourton. There was also a steam shed at this location to the right of the Freightliner terminal, but this closed in January 1967.
Author (3)

Wortley Junction (Leeds)

Then: 9 March 1961

This view of Fairburn 2-6-4T No 42093 heading a Bristol-Bradford (Forster Square) express was taken from the signalbox steps. The route from Leeds (Wellington) to Bradford (Market Street) was opened by the Leeds & Bradford Railway on June 1846. In the background is Holbeck Low Level station which opened in 1855 and closed in 1958. The bridge above the station carried the Great Northern main line into Leeds (Central), the two lines being connected by a spur, curving past Geldard box in the background. The sidings on the extreme right served the local gas works.

Now: 2 November 1994

With the closure of Central station in 1967 all traffic was transferred to Leeds City and, at the same time, a rationalisation of tracks approaching Leeds was carried out with a consequent closure of many of the old boxes. Wortley Junction box was demolished, so the current picture is taken from a footbridge now spanning the four tracks; the signalbox was originally situated at the end of the wall from where the lines to the gas works descended through the gate. By the time that this book is published, electric services will be operational but at the moment local services are formed of units such as this Class 144 No 144007 heading for Leeds on the 14.05 service from Skipton.

Author (2)

Calverley & Rodley

Then: 27 February 1960

This photograph was taken from the overbridge carrying the Leeds ring road. The station can be seen above the bridge in the background. The area possessed extensive sidings, which were used to store carriages during the winter months. A local Fowler '4F' No 44579 heads along the up slow line towards Leeds.

No: 2 November 1994

The current picture, showing West Yorkshire PTE Class 144 No 144023 working the 12.40 Leeds-Ilkley train, gives no indication of the extent of the railway in this area three decades ago.

Author (2)

Apperley Bridge

Then: Circa 1960
Opened one month after the line's opening in June 1846, this station was situated just west of the junction between the Leeds-Ilkley and Leeds-Keighley lines and just to the east of Thackley Tunnel. The picture shows clearly the island platform which separated the fast and slow lines. The fast lines usually accommodated the Bradford traffic, whilst the slow ones carried the trains for further north. The station clock shows 3.25pm, which would indicate that the train illustrated is the 3.15pm Leeds-Morecambe service, a train which ran at this period and which was usually worked by a Saltley-based 'Black 5' — in this case No 44812. The lamp indicates that the train was classed as a stopping service.
Now: 19 December 1994
The station, along with the other intermediate stations on this stretch of line (including Calverley & Rodley), closed on 20 March 1965. All signs of the station have now vanished as Class 156 No 156473 passes with the 12.49 Leeds-Carlisle service.
Eric Treacy/Author

Manningham

Then: 1959
A view of the shed and station at Manningham, one of two intermediate stations between Shipley and Bradford (Forster Square), sees two ex-L&YR 2-4-2Ts in excellent condition, albeit in store with Stanier 2-6-2T No 40112. By this date the use of the 2-4-2Ts on local services had ended with the introduction of DMUs. The shed buildings, in the form of a roundhouse, are in the top right-hand side of the picture. The shed originally opened in 1846, but was resited in 1872; amongst unusual locomotives shedded here were two ex-Caledonian Railway 0-4-4Ts in 1947/48. The station, visible on the left, opened in 1868.
Now: 19 December 1994
The shed was to close as late as 30 April 1967, whilst the station closed in March 1965. Also closed was Frizinghall, but this station has subsequently been reopened. Whilst the line remains and is currently being electrified, the shed yard is now an industrial estate.
Author (2)

Bradford (Forster Square)

Then: 12 March 1967
Originally named Market Street until 1924, the ex-Midland Railway terminus in Bradford at the end of the short branch from Shipley has been resited twice during its life, once in 1897 and again in 1990. The extensive sidings, both passenger and freight, are clearly visible in this photograph of Type 2 No D5228 (later No 25078 which was withdrawn in 1985) leaving with a train for Leeds as a Fairburn 2-6-4T heads for the sidings.

Now: 2 November 1994
Although long threatened with closure, Forster Square has never had its local services, to Ilkley and Skipton, withdrawn. However, with the contraction of the railways the surrounding area has become largely derelict. The station has been completely rebuilt and equipped for 25kV operation. Class 144 No 144002 is pictured leaving from the relocated station with the 12.01 train to Skipton. In the background can be seen the area of the old station platforms, now demolished, in use as the inevitable car park. Whilst there have been plans for yet another shopping complex on the site, the old siding area remains derelict.
Author (2)

Ingrow

Then: 3 June 1960
This suburb of Keighley once boasted two stations — the Midland station illustrated and Ingrow East on the Great Northern line to Queensbury (which closed on 23 May 1955). The Worth Valley branch opened on 13 April 1867 and Ivatt 2-6-2T No 41326, a regular locomotive on the branch at this time, is caught arriving at the station. There are a few passengers waiting for a trip up the valley.

Now: 9 January 1995
The branch closed on 30 December 1961 and was subsequently acquired for preservation by the Keighley & Worth Valley Light Railway. The station has been rebuilt since preservation and in the distance can be seen some of the sheds that house the fine collection of historic vehicles owned by the Vintage Carriages Trust. 'Jinty' No 47279 departs for Haworth and Oxenhope.
Author (2)

Oxenhope

Then: 15 August 1959
The history of the now famous Keighley & Worth Valley Railway has been told many times. Oxenhope is the terminus of the line, which originally opened on 13 April 1867 and continued in operation until 30 December 1961. Ivatt 2-6-2T No 41325 is at the terminus working the push-pull set.

Now: 8 January 1995
More than seven years after closure the line was to be reopened as a steam railway; more than a quarter of a century later the preserved railway has given pleasure to hundreds of thousands of passengers. It is considered by many to be the best preserved branch in the country. Today the station buildings remain externally the same, beautifully preserved, whilst the water tank and museum are new. The track and embankment are well maintained. 'Jinty' No 47279 is again seen, arriving with a service from Keighley.
Author (2)

Keighley Shed

Then: 15 May 1959
This view of the engine shed was taken from the signalbox at the north end of the station. The present Keighley station was built in 1883, with the platforms serving the Worth Valley and Great Northern lines curving away from those built for the main line. The shed was originally a sub-depot of Manningham, but reorganisation in 1935 saw it transferred to Skipton. On the shed is Fowler 0-6-0 No 44039, whilst Fairburn 2-6-2T No 42052 shunts empty stock. On the right is local 0-6-0T No 47419 shunting the freight yard.

Now: 19 November 1994
It is not possible to replicate exactly the earlier shot as the signalbox has long since vanished. The freight yard was closed in 1981 and now has a supermarket built on the site. Sprinter No 156468 passes the much denuded scene as it heads away towards Skipton with the 12.49 service from Leeds to Carlisle.
Author (2)

Grassington

Then: 6 October 1965
The branch from Embsay Junction, on the Skipton-Ilkley line, was opened on 29 July 1902. Regular passenger services were withdrawn as early as 21 September 1930, but the line continued to see freight and holiday specials until well after the end of World War 2. Skipton-based Standard Class 4MT No 75042 is shown ready to depart from the branch terminus with the local freight.

Now: 19 November 1994
Although the branch remains open as far as the limestone quarries at Rylstone, the line north of that point to Grassington closed completely on 9 August 1969. Today the station area is occupied by a housing estate. At least the author was able to explain to a local resident the reason for there being a lot of ballast to be found when digging in the garden!
Author (2)

Skipton South

Then: 30 September 1967

Skipton was once an important junction, with lines radiating to Colne, Hellifield, Grassington/Ilkley and Leeds. By the date of this photograph services over the Ilkley line had been withdrawn and the line remained only to serve Grassington branch freight. In the last year of BR steam operation, Type 2 No D5175 (later Class 25 No 25025 withdrawn in 1977) pilots Carnforth-based Class 9F 2-10-0 No 92118 on a Heysham-Hunslet oil train.

Now: 19 November 1994

The line south to Colne closed in 1970 and freight traffic over the Settle-Carlisle line has almost disappeared. Track reorganisation has just been completed, although the masts and catenary for the future electrification have yet to appear. Pacer Class 142 No 142058 arrives on the 13.01 service from Bradford (Forster Square) as Class 60 No 60002 *Capability Brown* waits in the new stabling point between duties on the Tilcon trains to and from Rylstone.

Author (2)

Skipton Station

Then: Undated
The tracks to the right are for the Ilkley/Grassington branch, which opened through to Skipton in late 1888. The Leeds & Bradford Railway originally reached Skipton in September 1848 with the extension of the line to Colne being opened in October the same year. The station in Skipton was resited in May 1876 on the opening of the Settle-Carlisle line. Stanier 2-6-4T No 42492 is ready to leave with a local stopping train to Garsdale; prior to 1959 these trains were normally extended to Hawes.

Now: 19 November 1994
The track layout around the station remained largely unchanged for decades until the second half of 1993 when major alterations were undertaken as part of the electrification scheme. As can be seen the station is well maintained, although the surrounding area was rather untidy during the alterations. West Yorkshire PTE Class 144 No 144009 departs with the 13.01 Leeds Morecambe train; currently there are just four return workings a day on the Morecambe line.

Eric Treacy/Author

Earby

Then: March 1955
The Skipton-Colne line of the Leeds & Bradford Railway opened on 2 October 1848 and the short branch to Barnoldswick in 1871. Stanier 2-6-4T No 42475 is pictured about to leave with a Skipton-Blackpool train.
Now: 18 November 1994
The line to Barnoldswick closed to passenger services on 27 September 1965 and to freight on 1 August 1966. The line from Skipton to Colne closed on 2 February 1970 and Earby station closed on the same date. As can be seen, all traces of the station have now gone and the trackbed has become a local pathway.
Ian Allan Library/Author

Gargrave

The: 6 August 1960
Lancaster-based 2-6-0 'Crab' No 42931 passes with an up Morecambe-Leeds train.
Now: 18 November 1994
The signalbox and yard have been removed, but the station remains in use, with about seven trains per day calling in each direction. Pacer No 142058 departs on the 09.01 Leeds-Morecambe service; unfortunately on this occasion no passengers either joined or got off the train. Although no garden now surrounds it, the 225 milepost still stands on the up platform.
D. Singleton/Author

Hellifield Shed

Then: Circa 1955
The shed was completed in 1880 and in 1910 28 locomotives were allocated to it, including two for snow clearing duties. Originally Hellifield had had two sheds, but that built by the L&YR closed in 1927 and its locomotives were transferred to the ex-Midland shed. In the 1940s there were around 30 locomotives shedded. Viewed from the platform can be seen a line of ex-LMS types, including two 'Crabs' and '8F' No 48159.

Now: 18 November 1994
The shed finally closed for operational purposes on 17 June 1963. After closure it was used to house some of the locomotives from the National collection, including the famous Gresley 'V2' No 4771 *Green Arrow*. After these locomotives departed the shed remained derelict until final demolition. As can be seen nothing now remains of the buildings.
Author (2)

Hellifield

Then: 25 June 1966
The railways reached Hellifield with the opening of the North Western Railway from Skipton northwestwards in 1849. In 1880 it became a busy junction with the opening of the L&YR line north from Blackburn. Its importance also grew with the development of traffic over the Settle-Carlisle line after its opening in 1876. A Derby Lightweight DMU, showing a Carlisle destination board, heads south past the station with the old bay platform for services to Blackburn (withdrawn in September 1962) behind. The shed, closed by this date but was still intact, can be seen on the right. The station was at this time in a reasonable state of repair, but gradually deteriorated until being boarded up in 1981.

Now: 18 November 1994
With the rundown of services over the past decades the station deteriorated even further until the point where the buildings were considered unsafe. The fact that £0.5 million was somehow made available from many sources to refurbish completely the buildings must surely be a small miracle, but that is what happened. Restoration work commenced on 24 January 1994 and by Friday 18 November the same year work had been completed and a reopening ceremony took place. The pair of 'Now' photographs were taken on this date and show Sprinter No 156438 making an unscheduled stop on the 08.56 service from Carlisle to Leeds. The train was conveying invited guests. The restoration is superb and well worth a visit when in the area.
Author (3)

Settle Junction

Then: 12 March 1966
The station at this point only remained in use for one year, from the opening of the Settle-Carlisle line in 1876 until the following year. Nevertheless it was still standing 90 years later when Holbeck-allocated Class 5 No 44854 passed on an up van train off the Morecambe line. The signalbox dates from 1913.

Now: 18 November 1994
The signalbox still stands, unlike the remains of the station, although the track layout has been altered as a result of a derailment on 2 May 1979 when the track was badly damaged. Sprinter No 156491 is passing on the 11.40 Carlisle-Leeds train; note that the current speed restriction on to the Morecambe line is 15mph, whereas in 1966 it was 45mph.
Author (2)

Clapham

Then: 12 March 1966
The Midland line from Skipton to Ingleton opened in 1849 and the following year Clapham became a junction with the opening of the line to Lancaster. Type 2 No D7592 (later Class 25 No 25242 withdrawn in 1984) rounds the curve with an up afternoon Morecambe-Leeds express. The line to Ingleton and Low Gill can be seen heading off north behind the train. Passenger services over the Low Gill route ceased in 1954 although goods traffic continued until March 1965. The line was also used for diversions off the West Coast main line, and Stanier Pacifics had been known to use it as well as a Gresley 'A4' on a special excursion.
Now: 18 November 1994
Today the station survives, although its role as the 'other' Clapham Junction is no more. The service over the line towards Morecambe has been reduced to four return workings a day which are operated by Pacers such as West Yorkshire PTE Class 144 No 144006. The unit is leaving with the 13.01 service from Leeds.
Author (2)

Wennington

Then: 12 September 1964
Holbeck 'Jubilee' No 45573
Newfoundland arrives on the 2.46pm
Morecambe Promenade-Leeds (City)
service which, at this time, was only
steam-hauled on Saturdays. In the
background is Fowler 2-6-4T
No 42359. The line to Lancaster
(Green Ayre) opened in 1849, whilst
that to Carnforth opened in June 1867
for passenger traffic.
Now: 24 January 1995
The signalbox still proclaims itself as a
junction, but this status ended more
than two decades ago. Passenger
services over the line to Lancaster
were withdrawn on 1 January 1966.
Pacer unit No 142096 is leaving on the
13.01 Leeds-Lancaster (Castle) train,
one of four daily services in each
direction currently to use the line.
N. A. Machell/Author

Morecambe

Then: 10 July 1968
Stanier Class 5 No 45231 hauls empty oil tanks past the junction to Heysham. Holt Bank Junction signalbox can be seen in the distance. The train would, of course, reverse down the branch (which opened in September 1904 and which was electrified as early as 1908). By this date steam operation on BR metals had only a few weeks to go. No 45231 was fortunately to pass into preservation, initially at Carnforth but now on the Great Central Railway at Loughborough.

Now: 24 January 1995
Sprinter No 150149 passes the junction as it approaches the new Morecambe station whilst working the 12.35 Heysham-Lancaster service. Currently there are only two passenger trains per day over the branch to Heysham on weekdays only.
D. Cross/Author

Morecambe Promenade

Now: 9 October 1965
The station was an imposing structure, which was opened to traffic in March 1907. Electric driving trailer No M29021 is on a three-car train of converted LNWR stock. These units had originally been built in 1914 to operate over the Willesden Junction-Earls Court route, but were converted for use on the Lancaster-Morecambe-Heysham services, commencing on 17 August 1953. They continued in use until withdrawal of the service on 1 January 1966.

Now: 24 January 1995
Today the old buildings still stand, although the rest of the former station site has been cleared for use as a car park. The old terminus was replaced by a new station, which opened in 1994. Unit No 150149 leaves on the 13.12 Lancaster-Heysham train. The old station buildings can be seen in the background.
Author (3)

Heysham

Then: 31 March 1963
The branch was opened in 1904 and, as can be seen in the picture of a Stanier Class 5 leaving with the Sunday morning 10.30am parcels train to Crewe, there were extensive sidings around the harbour.
Now: 24 January 1995
The sidings have all vanished with part of the land derelict and the rest either offices or car parks. Today there is just a single line into the station. Sprinter No 150149 is caught arriving with the 11.57 departure from Lancaster. One of the ferries, which still operate from the harbour, can be seen in the top left of the picture. The line on the bottom left is used by nuclear flask trains to Sellafield from the Heysham nuclear power station.
N. A. Machell/Author

Dent

Then: Undated
Opened in August 1877 Dent was one of the many intermediate stations over the Settle-Carlisle route that closed on 4 May 1970 with the withdrawal of local passenger services over the line. A departing southbound train has left one passenger on the platform.
Now: 19 January 1995
Comparison between the pictures suggests that it is the scenery rather than the railway that has changed. However, this is not the case as it was just starting to snow when the 'Now' picture was taken and the hills in the background vanished from view. The signalbox and the sidings are the most obvious changes, although the 11.40 service from Carlisle to Leeds produced nobody either alighting or boarding the train unlike the single passenger in the 'Then' shot. Whilst the station building is now in private hands, passenger services were restored on 14 July 1986.
Ian Allan Library/Author

Horton in Ribblesdale

Then: 23 May 1959
Carlisle Kingmoor-based Stanier Class 5 No 45100 heads a northbound freight past the box on the long climb to Blea Moor. The sidings on the right served the quarry. The station at Horton opened the same day as the Settle-Carlisle line itself, 1 May 1876.

Now: 17 December 1994
The quarry survives in operation although it is no longer rail served. The signalbox is another casualty as is the station which closed on 4 May 1970 along with all the other intermediate stations along the line, with the exception of Appleby and Settle. As with Dent services were restored in July 1986. Sprinter No 156480 is shown leaving the station on the 11.40 service from Carlisle to Leeds on a dismal December day.
Author (2)

Garsdale

Then: Undated

An ex-North Eastern Railway Class G5 0-4-4T waits in the branch platform with a train for Northallerton. When opened in August 1876 the station was originally known as Hawes Junction. The name board on the signalbox records the location as Garsdale Junction, but the station simply proclaims Garsdale.

Now: 19 January 1995

The through service to Northallerton was withdrawn in 1954, although the service to Hawes continued until March 1959. The branch has now been lifted. The station buildings have been altered and the signalbox is now only used in special circumstances. As with other intermediate stations, Garsdale closed on 4 May 1970 but was reopened 16 years later. The area has a reputation for being one of the wettest in the country, but on the day of the 'Now' photograph of Sprinter No 156498 arriving on the 10.49 train from Leeds to Carlisle, it was just starting to snow.

Ian Allan Library/Author

Appleby

Then: Undated

Opened on 1 May 1876, along with 14 other stations on the Settle-Carlisle line, Appleby was one of only two intermediate stations to survive the wholesale closure in May 1970.

Now: 19 January 1995

Although freight facilities were withdrawn in 1971, the station remains busy and is a credit to all those who look after it. It is kept in immaculate condition and has become very well known to enthusiasts and public when the steam specials call at the station to take water and, on rare occasions, carry out run pasts.

Appleby is a market town, but has developed as a tourist centre from which the railway benefits. Even on a cold January morning there were several passengers joining the train to Carlisle at 10.42. The water column and tower were renovated for use by steam specials by the local Round Table group.

Ian Allan Library/Author

Blackwell

Then: 7 July 1956

This station, situated on the Midland main line from Birmingham to Bristol was a favourite location for enthusiasts as it was situated at the north end of the famous Lickey Incline. Bristol (Barrow Road)-allocated Class 2P No 40426 is receiving plenty of attention from the assembled multitude as it heads south with a local Birmingham-Bristol service. This was always a busy location as the many banking locomotives used to gather at this point prior to returning down the bank to Bromsgrove for their next duty.

Now: 28 February 1995

The station at Blackwell closed on 18 April 1966 and, apart from Station Road, there is little to indicate that a station ever existed at this point. Today the scene is very different; bankers are a thing of the past as InterCity 125s, Class 158s and other modern DMUs climb the bank unassisted. The rear power car of the 12.00 Bristol-York service, No 43101 *Edinburgh International Festival*, is shown heading towards Birmingham (New Street).

Author (2)

Bromsgrove (bankers)

Then: 29 June 1957
A line up of banking engines await their next turn of duty. The locomotives concerned are '9F' No 92079, which is just visible, ex-GWR 0-6-0PTs Nos 8404 and 8410 and ex-LMS 'Jinty' No 47502. There was a small shed at Bromsgrove which housed, in 1959, 11 locomotives for use as bankers. These 11 comprised seven ex-GWR pannier tanks, one '3F' 0-6-0, two 'Jinties' and the one '9F'.

Now: 28 February 1995
Class 158 No 158821 passes by a speed on the 09.20 Swansea-Birmingham (New Street) service. The signalbox and the banking locomotives have disappeared, the latter being replaced by oil tanks serving a depot situated on the left of the picture. The shed closed in 1964.
Author (2)

Bromsgrove (south)

Then: Undated

As the Type 3 (later Class 37) No D6943 was new in September 1964, this photograph was probably taken in 1965. Stanier Class 8F No 48336 is taking water (to excess) after descending the bank with a heavy load of coal. the brakes would have been pinned down prior to the descent of the bank. The locomotive had stopped before reaching the water column and had, therefore, been uncoupled prior to running forward to take water.

Now: 28 February 1995

The Class 37 in the 'Then' photograph remains active, as No 37697, unlike the '8F'. Although there has been some rationalisation of track, the layout today remains similar. As one watches the Class 158s and InterCity 125s of today it is hard to believe what it used to be like getting a train up the 1 in 37 gradient towards Blackwell. The start of the gradient can just be seen top right as Class 37 No 37263 heads south towards Gloucester.

A. A. Vickers/Author

Evesham

Then: 2 June 1953

The Midland Railway first reached Evesham, a town also served by the Great Western line from Oxford to Worcester, with the opening of the line from Ashchurch on 1 October 1864. The line north from Evesham to Redditch opened in two stages in 1866 and 1868, thereby providing the MR with a diversionary route from Birmingham towards Ashchurch. The photographer of this picture obviously thought that the best way of celebrating the Coronation of HM Queen Elizabeth II was to take steam shots and here Ivatt 2-6-0 No 43013, with an ugly double chimney, takes more water than it needs before leaving with the 2.20pm all-stations service to Birmingham. Notice the Union Flags on the smokebox.

Now: January 1995

The ex-Midland route from Ashchurch to Redditch lost its passenger services on 17 June 1963, although buses had been substituted north of Evesham since 1 October 1962 due to the condition of the track. Freight services north of Evesham were also withdrawn in June 1963, and the final closure of the section from Evesham to Ashchurch came on 9 September 1963. Today the area of the station has been redeveloped for housing, although the old station buildings still stand and traces of the platform edge remain visible. Services over the Oxford-Worcester line continue.

E. Mitchell/J. Turner

Ashton-under-Hill

Then: Undated
This station was situated about half-way between Ashchurch and Evesham. The line through the station opened on 1 October 1864. Passenger services over the route were withdrawn on 17 June 1963.

Now: January 1995
Although the railway has long gone, the station remains and it is still possible to trace the platform edge. The station has been converted to a house and we are grateful to the owner for his permission to take this photograph.
Ian Allan Library/J. Turner

Ashchurch Junction

Then: 1950s
The livery of the coaches gives some clue to the date of this picture. The illustration shows well the layout at this once important country junction. To the left is the line to Great Malvern via Upton-on-Severn; in the centre is the main line north to Birmingham; and, branching off to the right, is the alternative route northwards via Evesham. Beyond the station was a line that linked the routes to Upton and Evesham; this line closed in 1957.

Now: 28 February 1995
The branch to Great Malvern lost its passenger services in two stages — from Upton-on-Severn to Great Malvern on 1 December 1952 and Ashchurch to Upton-on-Severn on 18 August 1961. The complete closure of this line came with the withdrawal of freight trains from Ashchurch to Tewkesbury on 2 November 1964. The line from Ashchurch to Evesham lost its passenger services on 17 June 1963 and freight over the line ceased three months later. A short section of the line remained to serve a private siding, but, judging from its condition, little traffic now uses it. Ashchurch station itself closed on 15 November 1971 and, as can be seen, there are now no traces of the platforms or buildings. An InterCity 125, comprising power cars Nos 43101 and 43103 with seven coaches, forms the 06.40 Newcastle-Bristol service. *W. A. Camwell/Author*

Upton-on-Severn

Then: August 1961
The branch from Ashchurch to Great Malvern opened in two stages. The link to Tewkesbury was completed as early as 1840, but the line thence to Great Malvern via Upton-on-Severn was not opened until 16 May 1864. Midland Class 3F No 43754 is pictured in the station with what appears to be a railtour. By this date, passenger services had already been withdrawn between Upton-on-Severn and Great Malvern and 14 August 1961 was to see passenger services withdrawn over the remainder of the branch to Ashchurch.
Now: December 1994
Freight services over the line from Tewkesbury to Upton-on-Severn were withdrawn on 1 July 1963. Today all traces of the railway have disappeared, to be replaced by an industrial estate.
Ian Allan Library/Author

Gloucester (Central)

Then: 15 July 1959
The Midland Railway originally had its own station in Gloucester, Eastgate, which was on the loop line from Tramway Junction to Tuffley Junction. The station and line were closed with the completion of the modernisation of the ex-GWR station at Gloucester — Central. Here an 'Austerity' 2-8-0 No 90066 passes through the ex-GWR station heading for the locomotive shed.
Now: 26 February 1995
Although the track layout remains, the surrounding area and the station have changed considerably. Class 158 No 158827 is pictured ready to leave on a Cardiff-Birmingham service, whilst, on the left, an InterCity 125 is caught on a diverted Paddington-Swansea turn.
N. Caplan/J. Turner

Haresfield

Then: 24 October 1964
This station was situated on the ex-Midland line south from Gloucester towards Bristol at the point where the ex-GWR and Midland lines ran parallel. There were, however, only platforms on the Midland line. The station dated originally from 1854. A stopping train (the 9.15am Bristol-Gloucester service), headed by Stanier Class 5 No 44965 of Saltley shed, arrives at the station.
Now: 26 February 1995
The station here closed on 4 January 1965 and, as a result, it was not possible to stand in exactly the same location so an adjacent overbridge was used to capture this shot of an InterCity 125 on the Sundays Only 14.05 Bristol-Edinburgh service. The power cars were Nos 43067 and 43162.
B. J. Ashworth/J. Turner

Thornbury

Then: 21 August 1963
The branch from Yate to Thornbury opened on 2 September 1872; passenger services were withdrawn as long ago as 19 June 1944 and, as a result, by the date of this photograph the branch was freight only. Bristol-based Class 4F No 44264 is seen at the terminus of the branch with a short freight.

Now: 26 February 1995
The freight service from Yate to Thornbury was officially withdrawn from 30 September 1967 and the line was subsequently demolished. However, the section from Yate to Tytherington was later relaid to serve a quarry; trains started running in 1972. No such reprieve for the section from Tytherington to Thornbury, however, and today there are no traces of the branch terminus. The street in the foreground is known as Midland Road, presumably in recognition of its former role.
M. J. Fox/J. Turner

Bristol (Engine Shed Sidings)

Then: 8 August 1964
A very dirty Stanier 'Jubilee' No 45602 *British Honduras* coasts past an adverse distant signal and a diesel shunter with the 9am Saturdays Only Paignton-Leeds express.

Now: 26 February 1995
There has been extensive redevelopment in the area and much of the former Midland Railway network in Bristol is a thing of the past. All traces of the original location have gone, so this picture is not exactly a comparison; it does show, however, the little that remains of the Midland presence in the city. What was the old main line is now nothing more than a long siding giving access to Avon County Council's waste transfer facility — which can just be seen through the bridge. In 1995 a train visits the line daily to collect containerised refuse for delivery to a reclamation site at Calvert in Buckinghamshire.
E. Thomas/J. Turner

Bath (Green Park)

Then: September 1952
This station was the terminus of the Midland's line from Bristol and also the northern terminus of the much-mourned Somerset & Dorset line south to Bournemouth. The Midland reached Bath in 1869 and the new station (only called 'Green Park' from 1951) was completed the following year. The Somerset & Dorset reached Bath in 1874. Ivatt 2-6-2T No 41243 is shown ready to depart from the station's impressive train shed.
Now: February 1995
Bath (Green Park) lost its passenger services on 7 March 1966 with the closure of the lines to Bournemouth and Bristol. The station then entered a period of uncertainty as to its future. Fortunately, like Manchester (Central) an alternative use was found for the building. The train shed now forms part of a carpark for a local supermarket and has been superbly restored.
Ian Allan Library/J. Turner

London, Tilbury & Southend Railway

The LT&SR was promoted jointly by the Eastern Counties and the London & Blackwall railways and operation was initially leased out. The first section of the line, from Forest Gate to Tilbury, opened on 13 April 1854. From Tilbury it was opened to Stanford-le-Hope (or Horndon as it was then called) later the same year. 1 July 1855 saw the line extended further, to Leigh, and thence on 1 March 1856 to Southend-on-Sea.

The line's London termini were Bishopgate and Fenchurch Street, the latter coming to predominate. Although Fenchurch Street opened in August 1841 and was one of the GER's London termini, it has always been traditionally associated with the LT&SR.

In 1875, on the expiry of the lease and the unwillingness of the GER to assume the line's operation, the LT&SR took over its own operation — a situation that was to last until 1912 when the company was taken over by the Midland Railway. The period between 1875 and 1912 was to witness dramatic changes to the fortunes of the LT&SR as massive suburban development in the Essex coastal corridor brought enormous increases in traffic.

The first stage of the LT&SR's further development occurred on 1 February 1884 with the opening of the extension eastwards from Southend to Shoeburyness. This was followed on 1 June 1888 with the opening of the Barking-Upminster-Pitsea cut-off route. Two branches were constructed to serve Upminster; that south to Grays (where it met the original route to Tilbury) opened on 1 July 1892 and that north to Romford (where it made a junction with the GER line) followed on 7 June 1893.

In order to relieve the pressure on Fenchurch Street, the Whitechapel & Bow line was jointly promoted with the District Railway and this section opened on 2 June 1902. This section of line was important in as much as it provided a direct link to the growing network of electrified underground lines. District Railway trains started to operate to East Ham in August 1905 and to Barking in April 1908. The section of the LT&SR from Campbell Road to Barking was quadrupled between 1905 and 1908.

Although the MR took over in 1912 with a promise of electrification, this was not to occur and steam continued to reign supreme through both the period of MR and LMS ownership. Electric services were, however, extended by the District Railway from Barking to Upminster in 1932 after an additional two tracks were laid between the points.

In 1948, the LT&SR passed initially to the London Midland Region. However, in the post-Nationalisation era it was clearly anachronistic for the LT&SR section to be divorced from the rest of the line's in Essex and a transfer of control in February 1949 saw the line transferred to the Eastern Region. It was, therefore, included as part of the Eastern Region's electrification proposals in the late 1950s. The plans envisaged the electrification of the original route, along with the Upminster cut-off and Upminster-Grays branch. Initially the line was electrified at 6.25kV between Fenchurch Street and one mile east of Barking and from Leigh to Shoeburyness, with 25kV being adopted for the remainder. First electric services were operated in November 1961 with the full service commencing on 18 June 1962. At this stage, the Upminster-Romford section was excluded, but this was to be included with the electrification scheme for the ex-GER main line to Norwich. Electric services between Romford and Upminster were inaugurated on 12 May 1986.

Although the entire LT&SR system survived until the 1980s, changing traffic patterns meant that the service to Tilbury Riverside was increasingly underused. The result was that the section serving the Riverside station was closed on 29 November 1992. At the time of writing the track is still *in situ*, although both it and the station look overgrown.

London (Fenchurch Street)

Then: Late 1950s

This London terminus dated originally from its opening by the London & Blackwall Railway on 2 August 1841. From 1850, until the opening of Broad Street, Fenchurch Street was also the terminus of North London Railway services and these were joined in 1854 by those of the LT&SR. Following the transfer of the ex-LT&SR lines from LMR to Eastern Region control in 1949, the lines were included in the Eastern's suburban electrification programme and work started in 1958. The last-built of Stanier's three-cylinder 2-6-4Ts, No 42536, passes under the signalbox and the newly erected catenary as it approaches the station.

Now: 16 January 1995

The signalbox has recently been removed and the electrified services now use 25kV rather than 6.25kV. The church with the spire, however, survives as Class 310/0 No 310051 heads into the station with the 13.05 from Shoeburyness.

Frank Church/Brian Morrison

Bromley by Bow

Then: August 1957
From Fenchurch Street to Gas Factory Junction, Bow, the LT&SR line used Great Eastern metals. The first station on LT&SR-owned track heading east was at Bromley by Bow. Fowler 2-6-4T No 42220 passes through the station with an up express. Note that work has yet to commence on the electrification of the line.

Now: 14 January 1995
Overhead electrification work meant that the station overbridge from which the 'Then' photograph was taken no longer exists and so it is not possible to achieve the same elevation. The hospital buildings in the background survive. Trains on the LT&S services no longer stop here and the platforms illustrated are disused. London Underground services on the adjacent District Line do, however, call at the station. Class 310/0 No 310075 is caught passing through the station with the 13.05 Shoeburyness-Fenchurch Street train.
Brian Morrison (2)

Barking

Then: 14 March 1952
An Ivatt Class 4MT 2-6-0 fitted with a double chimney, No 43031 of Derby, passes through the station heading an Orient Line boat train from St Pancras to Tilbury. Barking station originally only had two tracks, but the track was later quadrupled and modernisation followed with the electrification of the line to Upminster in 1932.

Now: 14 January 1995
A new road has been constructed across the station approach and the background buildings have changed together with the station nameboard. The 09.50 service from Fenchurch Street to Leigh-on-Sea slows for the scheduled stop formed of Class 310/0 No 310095.
P. J. Lynch/Brian Morrison

Upminster

Then: September 1932
Prior to the introduction of electric services between Barking and Upminster in September 1932, the track was tested by steam trains headed by a 4-4-2T. The LT&SR cut-off line from Barking, through Upminster, to rejoin the original line at Pitsea was opened on 1 June 1888.
Now: 14 January 1995
Considering that it is now 63 years since the 'Then' photograph was taken, very little has changed other than a revised track layout, the obvious demise of the semaphore signals and the demolition of the signalbox. On the far left can be seen the electrified lines of the LT&SR route, whilst a rake of London Underground 'D' stock approaches with a District Line service from Richmond.
Ian Allan Library/Brian Morrison

Grays

Then: 2 March 1958
This is one of the intermediate stations on the original LT&SR line that opened to Tilbury on 13 April 1854. A branch from Upminster to Grays opened on 1 July 1892. Here a Tilbury Riverside-Fenchurch Street train leaves Grays headed by Fairburn 2-6-4T No 42218.
Now: 14 January 1995
The background houses have gone together with the semaphore signals, whilst electrification masts abound and the bay platform and sidings gradually return to nature. Class 310/0 No 310077 leaves on the 10.02 service from Leigh-on-Sea to Fenchurch Street.
Frank Church/Brian Morrison

Grays (east)

Then: Undated
BR Standard Class 4MT 2-6-4T No 80074 is shown leaving with a train for Southend, which had been diverted. Many of these locomotives were allocated to the line during the last years of steam operation, replacing the ex-LT&SR 4-4-2Ts.
Now: 14 January 1995
A new and higher station footbridge has been constructed to allow for the overhead electrification, but little else of note has changed. Class 310/0 No 310086 passes over the level crossing controlled by East signalbox on the 09.50 service from Fenchurch Street to Leigh-on-Sea.
Frank Church/Brian Morrison

Tilbury Riverside (north)

Then: Undated
The LT&SR opened its line to Tilbury in April 1854. At Tilbury a triangular junction was formed with east and west curves heading to Tilbury Riverside terminus. The line beyond Tilbury to Stanford-le-Hope opened later in 1854. Viewed looking north, Stanier three-cylinder 2-6-4T No 42514 approaches the station from the west with a service from Fenchurch Street.
Now: 14 January 1995
The Tilbury Riverside branch was designed to provide a connection for the passenger traffic using Tilbury as a transhipment point for cruise ships and passenger sailings worldwide. With the decline of these services — few cruise ships now use Tilbury — passenger services over the Riverside branch were withdrawn on 29 November 1992. More than two years later the tracks are still in situ along with the overhead masts and catenary.
D. Sellman/Brian Morrison

Tilbury Riverside (south)

Then: 29 November 1992
The terminus at Tilbury Riverside was opened on 13 April 1854. The 'Then' photograph shows a view towards the buffer stops on the day that the station closed. The last scheduled passenger services ran over the branch on 28 November 1992, but two Network SouthEast specials were operated the following day. These were formed of Class 312/1 No 312788, which carried an appropriate headboard bearing the legend 'The Last Train Special from Tilbury Riverside'.

Now: 14 January 1995
Again just two years later, the tracks and electrification remain intact, although nature has started rapidly to take over.
Brian Morrison (2)

Pitsea

Then: 4 March 1961
The LT&SR section from Stanford-le-Hope to Leigh-on-Sea via Pitsea opened on 1 July 1855. The cut-off line from Pitsea, via Upminster, to Barking opened in June 1888. Stanier three-cylinder 2-6-4T No 42528 pauses at the station with a train to Fenchurch Street over the cut-off route via Laindon. The locomotive seems to have attracted the attention of the two boys on the platform.

Now: 6 January 1995
Very little seems to have changed in the 34 years since the 'Then' photograph, except for the replacement of the locomotives and rolling stock. Class 302s Nos 302217/226 restart from the station with the 14.35 service from Shoeburyness.
R. N. Jones/Brian Morrison

Westcliff

Then: 6 August 1960
The line beyond Leigh-on-Sea to Southend opened on 1 March 1856. The route east of Tilbury had originally been built as a single track section, but this was soon doubled. Stanier three-cylinder 2-6-4T No 42515 passes the station on the 12 noon working from Fenchurch Street to Shoeburyness.

Now: 6 January 1995
Today there is new platform lighting and, of course, the motive power is different. Otherwise the station appears to be in something of a time warp as so little has changed. Class 312/1s Nos 312787/785 enter the station on exactly the same working as that illustrated in the 'Then' shot — the 12.00 Fenchurch Street-Shoeburyness train.

G. M. Kichenside/Brian Morrison

Southend Central

Then: 7 August 1960
An excursion from Watford arrives in the station behind a Midland Class 4F 0-6-0 No 44348. The new signalbox is seen under construction behind the locomotive. Services to Southend Central began on 1 March 1856.
Now: 6 January 1995
Today the old signalbox has long gone and the platforms have been lengthened. Class 310/0s Nos 310049/088 arrive at the station with the 13.00 from Fenchurch Street to Shoeburyness train.
M. Edwards/Brian Morrison

Shoeburyness Shed

Then: 4 May 1958
A view from the London end of the platform shows the shed area more clearly. Various 2-6-4Ts can be seen, whilst one of Stanier's three-cylinder designs, No 42511, is pictured running round its train prior to returning to Fenchurch Street.
Now: 6 January 1995
Most of the yard on the right is now a car park, and the site of the shed has been sold and now forms an industrial complex. The platforms of the station have been lengthened and the whole view is now festooned with the trappings of electrification. In the platform is Class 302/0 No 302203 forming the 11.50 departure to Fenchurch Street.
Frank Church/Brian Morrison

Shoeburyness

Then: 1 June 1957
Southend Central was the terminus of the
LT&SR line until the extension to
Shoeburyness, was authorised in 1882, where
a school of gunnery had been established. The
line was opened on 1 February 1884. A
Fairburn 2-6-4T, No 42254, has just arrived at
the terminus with a train from London. The
photograph was taken from the back of the
buffer stops. Also visible, on the right, is the
locomotive shed that also opened in 1884.
Now: 6 January 1994
With the conversion to electric traction taking
place in 1962 the shed closed. The station
building is now revealed following the
demolition of the structure on the left in the
'Then' photograph, and the platforms have
been extended. Class 312 No 312730 departs
with the 10.50 service to Fenchurch Street.
Frank Church/Brian Morrison

Stratford upon Avon & Midland Junction

Although this company can lay claim to one of the longest names of all the railways that were to form the LMS in 1923 and the London Midland Region in 1948, it was also both one of the youngest and one of the most impecunious.

The S&MJR was formed in 1908 by an amalgamation of three local lines that served the area southeast and southwest of Stratford-upon-Avon. In chronological terms the oldest of the three was the East & West Junction Railway that was authorised in 1864 to build a link between Towcester, where it formed a junction with the Northampton & Banbury Junction Railway, and Stratford-upon-Avon. The line was opened between Fenny Compton and Kineton in 1871 and throughout on 1 July 1873.

This was followed by the Evesham, Redditch & Stratford-upon-Avon Junction Railway, which was authorised to construct a line from Stratford to Broom, on the Midland's Redditch-Evesham-Ashchurch route. This section was authorised in 1873 and was opened on 2 June 1879.

The final part of initial jigsaw was the Stratford-upon-Avon, Towcester & Midland Junction Railway, which was authorised to construct a line from Towcester east to the Midland's branch to Northampton at Ravenstone Wood Junction. This section was opened on 13 April 1891.

Almost from the start these three railways were impecunious and were run latterly by a joint committee appointed by the receivers. An act of 1901 allowed for the sale of the lines, but there were no takers and later that same decade, with debts increasing, an Act was obtained in 1908 to allow the three companies to merge as the Stratford-upon-Avon & Midland Junction Railway. The new company took over with effect from 1 January 1909.

In 1910 the railway was completed with the merger with the oldest N&BJR. This line had been opened between Blisworth and Towcester in May 1866 and between Towcester and Cockley Brake on 1 June 1872. The S&MJR was to retain its independence right through until the Grouping of the railways in 1923.

Without a doubt the line's most successful years were those during both world wars, when the line proved to be a useful route for freight traffic. In 1942 a south curve was installed at Broom as part of a plan to divert heavy freight away from the West Midlands. Another wartime development, which was to have a significant impact on the future history of the line, was the opening of an army depot at Burton Dassett, just west of Fenny Compton.

However, with the end of the war, harsh economic reality caught up with the S&MJR. The first section to lose its passenger services was that between Stratford-upon-Avon and Broom. Although services over this stretch were withdrawn on 16 June 1947, this closure was not made permanent until 23 May 1949. The section between Towcester and Cockley Brake (which was situated on ex-LNWR branch from Banbury to Buckingham lost its passenger services on 2 July 1951. The last section, from Blisworth to Stratford-upon-Avon retained passenger services until 7 April 1952.

Despite the loss of passenger services, freight continued to be important over much of the route. Two sections did, however, lose their freight services during the 1950s — Towcester-Cockley Brake on 29 October 1951 and Towcester-Ravenstone Wood Junction (on 30 June 1958). The continuing importance of the line was reflected, in 1960, by its selection as one of the main routes for the transfer for iron ore from Banbury to South Wales. This decision led to the construction of a new curve at Stratford to enable trains to reach the Honeybourne line, the reorientation of the junction at Fenny Compton as well as the complete closure of the line west of Stratford to Broom. This section was to close on 13 June 1960.

However, despite the changes the decline in freight from the ex-Great Central main line (which was also being run down) and the gradual decline in the iron ore traffic meant that the remainder of the S&MJR was to succumb during the 1960s, with the exception of the line from Fenny Compton to the Ministry of Defence base at Kineton. The line from Blisworth to Byfield (where a connection was made with the Great Central main line) was closed completely on 3 February 1964. This was followed on 1 March 1965 by the closure of the Burton Dassett-Stratford-upon-Avon line and, in June 1965, by the closure of the Byfield-Fenny Compton route. The link at Byfield to the ex-GCR main line remained open until later the same year. The final withdrawal occurred in September 1967 when the remaining spur at Blisworth, which had survived to give access to an industrial siding, was closed.

This meant that the only section remaining was that between Fenny Compton and the MoD base; this was transferred to MoD ownership on 19 July 1971. Ironically, however, the bulk of the traffic at the time of writing over this remaining part of the S&MJR is represented by locomotives and rolling stock from British Rail being transferred to the base for secure storage.

Stratford upon Avon

Then: 1930

Stratford upon Avon was the headquarters of the S&MJR and was reached by the company in 1873. Until the completion of its own station in 1876, the railway used the existing GWR station in the town. The section west of Stratford was opened in 1879. The shed also dated from 1876. This view shows the shed on the right with LMS 0-6-0s out-shedded from Saltley. The lines to the left joined to the GWR and those on the right headed towards Broom, where the S&MJR met the Midland Railway's Evesham-Redditch line.

Now: January 1995

The section from Stratford to Broom lost its passenger services as early as 16 June 1947 (although this was not made permanent until two years later). The section from Stratford to Blisworth was to succumb on 7 April 1952. Freight services were, however, to last longer, being withdrawn from Broom to Stratford on 1 June 1960 and from Stratford to Burton Dassett on 1 March 1965. As can be seen, all traces of the railway line have been eliminated.

Ian Allan Library/J. Turner

Ettington

Then: August 1957

This was the first station east of Stratford on the S&MJR. The line through the station opened in 1873 and it formed part of a cross-country link between the Midland at Broom and the LNWR at Blisworth and the Midland at Ravenstone Wood Junction, near Northampton. By the time of this photograph, passenger services, which had been withdrawn on 7 April 1952, were a thing of the past, but the line remained open for freight.

Now: January 1995

Ettington continued to receive freight until facilities were withdrawn in November 1963. The line was closed completely on 1 March 1965 and was subsequently lifted. Although it is difficult to see through the dense undergrowth, the station buildings still stand more than three decades after final closure.

Ian Allan Library/J. Turner

Kineton

Then: August 1957
By the date of this photograph, Kineton station had been closed to passengers for five years, passenger services having been withdrawn on 7 April 1952. The line, however, remained at this date an important freight artery. Despite its closure, the station remains in good condition and there is evidence of the freight traffic that country stations like this could generate in an era when British Railways was still legally a common carrier.

Now: December 1994
Freight facilities were withdrawn from the station in November 1963 and the line closed completely two years later. Three decades on you would be hard pressed to realise that there was once a station on this site; light industry now dominates the scene.
Ian Allan Library/J. Turner

Byfield

Then: 1951
This was the first station east of Fenny Compton on the line eastwards towards Blisworth. The line opened in 1873 but Byfield achieved greater importance when a link was built to connect the S&MJR with the new Great Central. Midland '4F' No 44186 pauses with a single-coach train at the station. There would appear to have been some custom for the station. A freight passes through on the other line.

Now: January 1995
Passenger services were withdrawn on 7 April 1952 and, following the gradual decline of the Great Central, freight services over the line to Fenny Compton succumbed in 1965. Today the station site has completely reverted to nature and has been converted into a pocket park.
Ian Allan Library/J. Turner

Fenny Compton

Then: 1951
This was the point where the S&MJR met the
Great Western's main line from Banbury to
Birmingham. The S&MJR reached this point in
1871 with the opening of the line to Kineton —
the first part of the line to be completed. At this
date passenger services were still using the
station on trains between Stratford and
Blisworth, but its days were numbered.
Now: January 1995
Although it was not possible to replicate the
'Then' photograph exactly, it is possible to see
the remains of the ex-S&MJR station. The line
to Kineton remains open to serve an MoD
depot at Burton Dassett; ironically, much of
the traffic these days is in BR rolling stock,
both new and surplus, being stored securely at
the depot. Note the replacement signalbox and
the surviving lower quadrant signal.
Ian Allan Library/J. Turner

Cheshire Lines Committee

Serving the area between Manchester, Liverpool and Chester, the Cheshire Lines Committee came into being on 5 July 1865 when the interests of the Great Northern and Manchester, Sheffield & Lincolnshire railways were combined. The partners in the CLC were increased on 18 July 1866 by the involvement of the Midland Railway.

The initial elements of the CLC comprised four lines in south Manchester/north Cheshire that were authorised in the early 1860s. These were the Stockport & Woodley Junction Railway (authorised to link Stockport with Woodley and opened on 12 January 1863), the Cheshire Midland Railway (authorised to link Altrincham with Northwich and opened from to Knutsford on 12 May 1862 and thence to Northwich on 1 January 1863), the West Cheshire Railway (authorised to link Northwich with Helsby and opened on 1 September 1869) and the Stockport, Timperley & Altrincham Junction Railway (authorised to link Stockport with the LNWR line at Broadheath and with the MSJAR at Altrincham and opened in 1865-66). Also incorporated in the CLC at this stage were two lines in Liverpool — the line between Liverpool (Brunswick Dock) and Garston (which had opened on 1 June 1864) and the authorised extension into Liverpool (Central) which was authorised in 1864 and opened 10 years later.

The expansion of the CLC continued from the mid-1860s onwards. The line linking Godley and Woodley at the committee's eastern extremity passed to it in 1866; a branch from Cuddington (on the Northwich-Helsby line) to Winsford opened on 1 June 1870 and the Manchester-Cressington Junction via Warrington line opened 1873. Initially CLC services ran to Manchester (London Road) but services were diverted to a temporary station at Manchester (Central) on 9 July 1877 with the permanent station being opened on 1 July 1880.

Further expansion saw the authorisation of the Chester & west Cheshire Junction Railway to link Mouldsworth (on the Northwich-Helsby line) via Mickle Trafford to Chester. A new station, Northgate, was provided at Chester. The line opened on 2 November 1874. On Merseyside, the North Liverpool Lines, from Hunt's Cross/Halewood to Walton-on-the-Hill and Aintree were opened on 1 December 1879 with the extension to Liverpool (Huskisson) following on 1 June 1880. The latter lost its passenger services as early as 1 May 1885. In Warrington, the main Liverpool-Manchester route was straightened thereby avoiding Warrington (Central) station and

thus allowing an acceleration of services. This section of line opened on 13 August 1883. The last significant opening occurred on 1 September 1884 with the inauguration of services on the Southport & Cheshire Lines Extension Railway line between Aintree and Southport (Lord Street).

At the Grouping in 1923 the CLC retained its independence. The legislators felt that by allocating the committee to either the LMS or the LNER would seriously disadvantage commercially the other. As a result the CLC retained its independence through until Nationalisation. During the interwar years, there were few major changes, although the Winsford branch lost its passenger services on 1 January 1931 (it was to close completely on 1 September 1958).

Since Nationalisation much of the erstwhile CLC has succumbed to the elimination of duplicate routes, but much also survives. Although both Liverpool (Central) and Manchester (Central) are no more, the line from Cressington Junction to Cornbrook Junction still carries passenger services, as does the line southwards from Altrincham through Northwich to Chester, although Northgate closed on 6 October 1969 and services were diverted to General.

Amongst the casualties, the first to succumb was the line north from Aintree to Southport, which lost its passenger services on 7 January 1952. Passenger services were withdrawn from the line from Aintree to Gateacre on 7 November 1960 and thence to Hunt's Cross on 17 April 1972. The line from Hunt's Cross to Huskisson Goods was to close completely on 31 August 1976. The line between Glazebrook and Godley via Stockport progressively lost its passenger services in the early 1960s, but the route survived as a freight line intact until the 1980s and, indeed, with the arrival of the Manchester Metrolink tramway system in the early 1990s passenger services were restored over the Altrincham-Northenden Junction section. Three sections of the freight-only route have, however, succumbed. The Cheadle Junction-Portwood section closed *circa* 1980, that between Partington and Glazebrook in August 1982 and that between Portwood and Bredbury *circa* 1986. Much of the site of Stockport (Tiviot Dale) station has now completely disappeared.

Of all the surviving relics of the CLC none is, perhaps, more impressive than Manchester (Central) station. Following closure on 5 May 1969 the station was long threatened. However, it survived and has now been very successfully transformed into the G-Mex conference and exhibition centre.

Southport (Lord Street)

Then: 29 July 1921
The Cheshire Lines Committee, encouraged to extend northwards to serve Southport, was authorised in 1881 and 1882 to construct a line from Aintree to Southport. It opened on 1 September 1884. Lord Street became the CLC's terminus in the town. This is a general view of the station taken shortly before it closed completely.

Now: 31 December 1994
The CLC line to Southport was a relatively early casualty and the station at Lord Street closed completely on 7 January 1952. After use for a period as a bus station, the site has now become occupied by the ubiquitous supermarket — a fate shared by many other station sites.
J. Garth/Author

Skelton Junction

Then: 13 April 1966
The signalbox here once controlled a very busy junction. The line to the left joined the LNWR route through to Warrington Arpley, that in the middle headed northwards to join the main CLC route from Warrington to Manchester at Glazebrook Junction, whilst that on the right curved away to join the Altrincham line at Deansgate Junction. A Stanier '8F' heads down this last named line with a freight.

Now: 31 May 1993
The line to Glazebrook was closed north of Partington on 3 August 1982, whilst the line towards Warrington Arpley closed on 8 July 1985. Passenger services were reinstated over the Skelton Junction-Stockport line when services to Manchester from Chester were diverted following the closure of the Manchester-Altrincham line for conversion to Metrolink operation on 24 December 1991.

J. R. Hillier/Author

Clan 37 No 37421, now named *The Kingsman,* heads the diverted 13.30 Holyhead-Manchester Victoria on 31 May 1993.

Altrincham

Then: 2 April 1971

Altrincham, apart from being used by CLC trains operating southwards towards Chester, was also the terminus of the Manchester, South Junction & Altrincham Railway, which was jointly owned by the LNWR and Great Central. It was in 1931 that the 8.5 miles between Manchester and Altrincham was electrified using 1,500V dc. The three-car sets introduced in 1931 were to last until the route was converted to 25kV operation in 1971. One of the 1,500V units, No M28581, is seen entering the station with a service from Manchester. The Altrincham line was the first in the country to utilise 1,500V dc.

Now: 30 January 1995

Although British Rail services continue to use the station as part of the Manchester-Stockport-Altrincham-Chester route, the MSJ&A part of the station is now operated by the new Manchester Metrolink. British Rail services over the line were withdrawn on 24 December 1991 and the new Metrolink services were inaugurated on 15 June 1992. One of the Italian-built trams, No 1015, approaches the station from the north.

A. W. Hobson/Author

Northwich

Then: 20 August 1955
The Cheshire Lines Committee route through Northwich from Knutsford to Northwich opened on 1 January 1863, from Northwich to Helsby on 1 September 1869 and from Mouldsworth to Chester on 2 November 1874. Stanier Class 8F No 48500 heads an empty ICI hopper train past the station *en route* back to Peak Forest as 'O4/1' 2-8-0 No 63743 waits to leave the yard. Situated at the heart of the Cheshire salt industry, Northwich was an important intermediate point and a steam depot was located here, just to the left of the picture, to service the many freight locomotives required.

Now: 30 January 1995
Northwich remains an important intermediate station served by Manchester-Chester trains. Regional Railways Class 101 DMU set No 101679 departs from the station forming the 13.00 service from Chester to Southport. The shed was closed in 1968 and the site is currently being redeveloped.

Brian Morrison/Author

Manchester (Central)

Then: 23 March 1973

This superb station, which originally was the Manchester terminus of the CLC, was opened in 1880. The train shed, with a span of 210ft, was only 30ft narrower than the Midland's terminus in London, St Pancras. The station closed on 5 May 1969, some four years before this photograph was taken, and at this stage its future was uncertain.

Now: 2 February 1995

Fortunately, unlike elsewhere (most notably with Bradford Exchange, Birmingham Snow Hill and Birkenhead Woodside), the opportunity that the train shed offered for sensible redevelopment was taken, with the result that Manchester gained an excellent exhibition hall — the G-Mex Centre. More recently, the Manchester Metrolink network was extended past the old station *en route* to Altrincham. The tracks of the new tramway can be seen heading up the ramp adjacent to the hall prior to joining the old railway formation out of the station.
P. E. B. Butler/Author

Stockport (Tiviot Dale)

Then: May 1960

Originally opened on 1 December 1865, Stockport (Tiviot Dale) was situated on the CLC line from Woodley to Altrincham. Although more centrally placed than the rival LNWR station, Edgeley, Tiviot Dale was always the poor relation. Here we seen Class 5 No 44856 waiting to depart on the 4.52pm stopping train to Derby.

Now: 5 February 1995

Passenger services to Tiviot Dale were withdrawn on 2 January 1967 and the line was closed completely between Bredbury and Portwood in the mid-1980s; the track was lifted from 1986 onwards. In spite of help from a local, who assured me that I was standing in the correct position to duplicate the 'Then' picture, I am not 100% certain. The ornate top to the tower in the background is about the only recognisable feature. The M63 motorway now runs in the background and the river underneath has been slightly diverted. I got to the spot just in time as the demolition team was busy at work and, as can be seen , plenty of track was in evidence. In a few months no trace will remain of the railway at this location other than the blocked-off tunnel entrance in the hill.
J. R. Bardsley/Author

Lancashire & Yorkshire Railway

Formed in 1847, the origins of the 'Lanky' dated back to the opening of the first stretch of the Manchester & Leeds Railway. This line was first promoted in the mid-1830s and was opened between Manchester and Littleborough on 3 July 1839. The section on the east of the Pennines, from Hebden Bridge to Normanton (where the line met the North Midland Railway) followed on 5 October 1840. The missing section, including the one mile 125yd-long Summit Tunnel, was opened on 1 March 1841. Initially M&LR ran to Oldham Road station in Manchester, but, even before the line was opened throughout, the company had obtained powers to build a link to meet an extension of the Liverpool & Manchester Railway and to build a new station — later to be called Victoria.

In Yorkshire the M&LR promoted a link from Greetland to Halifax (Shaw Syke) which opened on 1 July 1844. This was followed by the completion of the line from Mirfield to Low Moor, which was opened on 12 July 1848. It was not until 1850 that the lines from Low Moor to Bradford and from Low Moor to Halifax were completed. Two years later the direct line from Sowerby Bridge to Halifax was opened. By this date the M&LR had become the Lancashire & Yorkshire and its importance in the region was growing. The extension beyond Wakefield to Goole (which gave the L&YR access to the Humber estuary and the lucrative trade to be derived from the shipping of coal) was opened in 1848 whilst the line between Horbury and Barnsley followed in 1850. Also opened in 1850 was the line from Huddersfield to Penistone. Apart from the main lines, the L&YR also operated a number of branches in the area, to Rishworth, Stainland, Meltham, Holmfirth and Clayton West.

Back in Lancashire, the L&YR created a complex network of lines serving the area north of Liverpool and Manchester. One of the most important elements in this network (and originally a bitter competitor of the L&YR) was the East Lancashire Railway which was merged with the L&YR in 1859. The ELR built a number of lines, including those linking Manchester with Bury (1846), Blackburn with Preston (1846), Accrington with Blackburn (1848), Stubbins Junction with Accrington (1848), Accrington with Burnley (1848) and Burnley with Colne (1849). Elsewhere in Lancashire major lines that were opened included those promoted by the Liverpool & Bury Railway (1848), the Blackburn, Darwen & Bolton (1848), the Liverpool, Ormskirk & Preston (1849 — by which date it had merged with the ELR) and the Liverpool, Crosby & Southport (1850).

The L&YR's first reached Preston through its part ownership of the North Union Railway, which formed the West Coast main line south from Preston. At Preston, the struggling Preston & Wyre Railway, which had opened a line to Fleetwood in 1840, was taken over by the L&YR in conjunction with the LNWR. This established the joint ownership of the railways on the Fylde peninsula and the first line to Blackpool was opened in November 1846.

Although the L&YR's early reputation was poor, by the later years of the 19th century it had established a strong local tradition. It was to prove itself innovative in its early adoption of electric traction and commercially astute in its development of shipping services. It was, however, destined not to reach the Grouping in 1923 as an independent company; it merged with the LNWR the previous year. The interwar years saw passenger services withdrawn from a number of the lesser branches, such as those to Rishworth and Stainland, but the bulk of the network passed to British Railways in 1948.

Since Nationalisation there has been the inevitable rationalisation of services. All the Yorkshire branches have been closed completely, although that to Clayton West only closed as recently as 1983. Through passenger services over the Calder Valley main line east of Sowerby Bridge have also disappeared. However, passenger trains continue to operate from both Burnley (having been restored) and Manchester to Bradford via Halifax, from Huddersfield to Penistone, from Wakefield to both Barnsley and Goole. On the west of the Pennines, the line from Colne to Preston remains, as does the line from Poulton to Blackpool North and that to Blackpool South. The direct line to Blackpool Central along with the line to Fleetwood have both, however, disappeared. The latter survives in part for freight only use, as does the stub of the Longridge branch. The lines linking Liverpool to Southport, to Preston via Ormskirk and that to Bury via Wigan as far as Bolton also survive. The line from Southport to Preston has, however, been closed completely. The line north of Blackburn to Hellifield, which was retained for freight use and for diverted passenger services has seen a partial reintroduction of scheduled passenger services. Elsewhere, although the lines north from Bury to Accrington and to Rawtenstall/Bacup/Rochdale have all closed, the preserved East Lancashire Railway has now reopened the stretch from Bury to Rawtenstall and is currently working to complete the reopening of the line from Bury to Heywood, where it will connect with the BR freight-only line to Castleton. Finally, although it is still operated, the line from Manchester to Bury is now part of the Manchester Metrolink system and ownership has passed to the Metrolink consortium.

Holmfirth

Then: 26 September 1959
The first train left Holmfirth on 1 July 1850. The branch was only about 1½ miles long to its junction with the Huddersfield-Penistone line at Brockholes. The station was a fine building in mock-Gothic style. A turntable was installed by the L&YR in 1883. Traffic steadily declined after World War 2 and closure eventually came as the end of October 1959. Only one month before closure, local Fowler 2-6-4T No 42413 is ready to return to Huddersfield; this was one of the locomotives to operate the service on the last day of operation.

Now: 26 November 1994
The fine station is still in a good state of repair, but the trackbed has completely vanished. The photograph was taken from the car park of the hall of the local Jehovah's Witnesses, whilst behind the photographer was a private house and grounds.
Author (2)

Wakefield Shed (25A/56A)

Then: 24 August 1961

Wakefield was one of the largest sheds on the L&YR and opened in 1867 with an allocation of around 60 locomotives. Local 'WD' 2-8-0 No 90109 heads an empty rake of coal wagons back to the collieries past the former coal stage and water tower. The cooling towers of the local power station can just be seen, as can the last L&YR survivors — two 0-6-0s — at the depot, albeit in store. The signals in the distance control Calder Bridge Junction, once a very busy site. In the latter years of steam operation ex-LNER 'B1s' and 'J50s', amongst others, were allocated to the shed. It finally closed on 3 June 1967, but was then used as a wagon repair depot for several years.

Now: 5 August 1994

It is only relatively recently that the depot was finally demolished, but happily the bridge to the entrance still survives with very limited access. The power station is also being demolished. The line is still mainly freight, but a Pacer service from Wakefield to Pontefract passes nearly every hour. This service has only recently been reintroduced after a gap of some 20 years. Passing in the evening sunshine is Class 37/7 No 37706 *Conidae* with a rail train from Castleton.

Author (2)

Horbury and Ossett (East)

Then: 13 July 1958
This once extremely busy section of
quadruple track has now been rationalised.
The picture shows well all the various crossovers at this point as well as the lines trailing
off to the left which used to form the third
side of the triangle from Horbury Junction to
Crigglestone on the Wakefield-Barnsley
line. Ivatt 2-6-0 No 46437 heads the 12.8pm
Mirfield-Goole stopping train into the very
deep cutting.

Now: 29 November 1993
It is only within the last three years that the
tracks have been reduced to one up and one
down and the junction removed. The line is,
however, still connected at the Crigglestone
end as a dead-end siding; it is used
occasionally for special duties. Now a
common sight, Class 60s are used on many
merry-go-round workings from Fiddlers
Ferry power station to the Selby coalfield.
No 60044 *Ailsa Craig* performs on one of
these duties and will return within two to
three hours on a loaded train.
C. W. Bendall/Author

Horbury and Ossett (West)

Then: January 1960
This photograph was taken prior to the reorganisation of the trackwork which occurred upon the building of the massive marshalling yard at Healey Mills in 1963. The yard was designed to handle the vast amount of wagon load traffic still crossing the Pennines in the early 1960s as well as for local coal traffic before the introduction of merry-go-round trains. The yard is situated to the rear of the photographer. The station was on the other side of the road bridge in the distance and closed in 1961. Normanton-based Stanier 2-6-2T No 40179 heads west on an all-stations stopping service to Sowerby Bridge; this would connect with an express to Manchester Victoria.
Now: 28 November 1994
The 12.25 Wakefield Westgate-Manchester Victoria Pacer No 142028 takes the yard avoiding line. This hourly service (via Huddersfield) is the only one currently to use the line and has been under threat for many years; it does, however, provide a useful connecting service with the Leeds-King's Cross trains. The old wagon works on the left now have different functions, whereas the shed on the right is still employed for repairs. Few freights still visit the yard, much of which has been taken out of use and the remains employed as a permanent way centre. Crew changes are still undertaken alongside the old depot for trans-Pennine work.
K. Smith/Author

Thornhill Junction/Ravensthorpe

Then: 20 June 1960
This is the point where the L&YR Calder Valley route meets the ex-LNWR Leeds-Manchester line. From this point the companies' lines ran alongside each other for 2½ miles until Heaton Lodge Junction. The station visible is Ravensthorpe, which opened in 1869 and remains in use. To the left of the picture there was Thornhill power station, which has now been demolished. Stanier 2-6-2T No 40075 is shown passing whilst working a Normanton-Sowerby Bridge local train.

Cleckheaton Central

Then: 20 August 1959
More than adequate motive power in the form of Holbeck (Leeds)-based Standard '5MT' No 73169 is seen at the head of a local stopping train as it enters the station *en route* towards Mirfield. The passenger service ceased in June 1965, 117 years after the line was opened in 1848.

Now: 28 November 1994
As can be seen the junction has been simplified and the speed limit raised. The station buildings are an example of a timber-built 19th century LNWR station and are listed. The buildings on the down side became damaged and were replaced with a standard bus shelter, whilst the remaining buildings on the up side have been offered to any railway preservation organisation or any other body willing to provide them with a new home.

One of West Yorkshire PTE's Class 158s, No 158904 in maroon livery, heads towards Dewsbury and Leeds on the 10.28 Manchester Airport-York service.
Author (2)

Now: 16 November 1994
As can be seen, nature has taken over the site, but amongst the undergrowth the track still remains. For many years there have been plans to reopen the line as part of a museum project based at Low Moor to provide a link with Heckmondwike. As a result the track was not lifted after the route's final closure. The line crossed the M62 motorway and this involved the construction of an expensive bridge — a bridge which probably never carried more than 100 trains. The transport museum is currently under construction at Low Moor, but little appears to be developing with regards to the tramway.
Author (2)

Brighouse station

Then: 12 July 1960
The 10.30am Liverpool Exchange-
Newcastle service arrives at Brighouse
hauled by one of the regular Bank Hall
(27A) 'Jubilees' No 45717 *Dauntless*,
which appears to have used little coal
from Liverpool. Brighouse station opened
in 1840 and remained open until
3 January 1970, since when the line has
been mainly freight only.
Now: 18 December 1994
West Yorkshire PTE has had plans to
reintroduce a service from Bradford to
Huddersfield and reopen the station,
which would help to ease the congested
roads but plans have not been finalised.
The service over the Standedge route had
been diverted on this Sunday due to
engineering work, which was the reason
for Class 158 No 158804 passing on the
10.58 Newcastle-Liverpool train.
Author (2)

Greetland

Then: 14 July 1959
This was the junction for the line which branched off the Calder
Valley main line to climb a steep bank at 1 in 44.5 across the
River Calder to reach Halifax. Initially, when opened in 1844,
the line served Halifax Shaw Syke, which was a little way to the
west from the site of the current station. Greetland station
opened, as a result, in 1844 and lasted until September 1962. It
was primarily served by trains from Normanton to Sowerby
Bridge and from Huddersfield to Halifax and Bradford. It was
also the junction station for the Stainland branch, which lost its
passenger services in 1929. The modern signalbox is in sharp
contrast to the station building and the lines to Halifax can be
seen trailing off to the left as Stanier 2-6-2 No 40140 leaves for
Sowerby Bridge.
Now: 16 November 1994
All signs of the station are gone, but the signalbox remains
intact but unused. The line up the bank to Halifax is still *in situ*
although no traffic has used it since 1988. West Yorkshire PTE
has expressed the wish to re-establish rail services from
Bradford to Huddersfield via Halifax and reopen some
intermediate stations. This proposed service would use this
currently mothballed section of track. The new route would
provide a very much faster service than the buses could offer
and would probably generate a lot of traffic. However, in the
current climate of uncertainty little progress has been made.
Author (2)

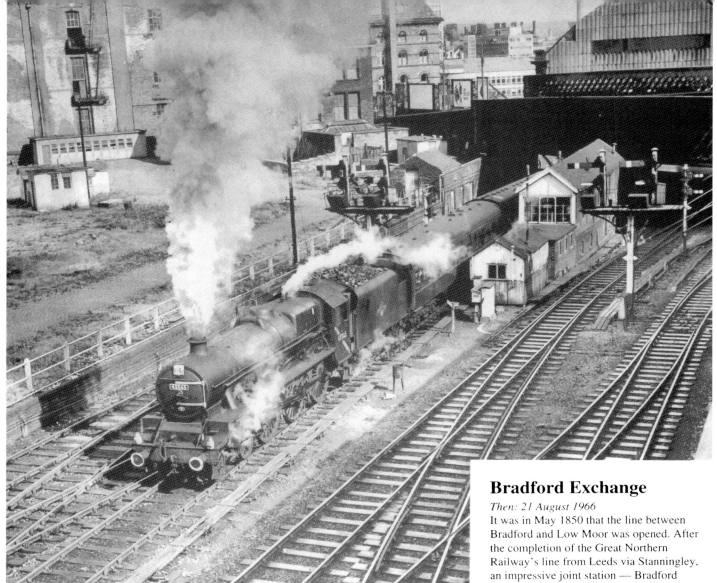

Bradford Exchange

Then: 21 August 1966
It was in May 1850 that the line between Bradford and Low Moor was opened. After the completion of the Great Northern Railway's line from Leeds via Stanningley, an impressive joint station — Bradford Exchange — (shared by the L&YR and the GNR) was constructed in the 1860s. It was situated at the bottom of a 1 in 50 climb to Bowling Junction, which involved many trains being banked.

'Jubilee' No 45565 *Victoria*, allocated to Low Moor, leaves Exchange with an excursion to Blackpool. The station roof can be seen above the bridge. The station was taken out of use on 15 January 1973 when remaining services were transferred to the first platforms of the new station.

Now: 2 November 1994
The new Exchange station (later rechristened 'Interchange') was built about 400yd further up the bank on the south side of the Bridge Street bridge. The first two platforms were opened in January 1973, with the remaining two platforms being constructed after the closure of the original station. The fully integrated road/rail station was not completed until March 1977 when it was opened by the then Secretary of State for Transport, William Rodgers. The railway was originally in a tunnel at this point, but this was opened out *circa* 1873.

The view shows the modern station in the foreground and the bus interchange on the left. Also visible is the ex-railway owned Victoria Hotel.
Author (2)

187

Low Moor station

Then: 5 April 1959
The photograph shows the Sunday Pullman from Harrogate arriving from Leeds Central headed by 'B1' 4-6-0 No 61214 and 'Crab' 2-6-0 No 42863. The train had been diverted via Low Moor due to engineering work between Leeds and Wakefield and had travelled via the Bradford avoiding line, from which the Eastern Pacifics were banned. As a result locomotives were changed at Low Moor, this pair giving way to Copley Hill-based 'A1' No 60117 to take the train forward via Cleckheaton, Horbury and Wakefield Kirkgate before joining the main line at Hare Park Junction. This busy station was opened in 1848 and finally closed on 12 June 1965.

Now: 19 December 1994
This picture was taken from the road bridge which used to be above the station. An incredible transformation has taken place in the area; all signs of the station, locomotive depot and extensive marshalling yards have completely vanished. Class 158 No 158904, on the 10.53 Selby-Manchester Victoria service, passes silently past the point where the station used to be. In the background can be seen the buildings being constructed for the future West Yorkshire Transport Museum.

Author (2)

Low Moor (west)

Then: 7 July 1959
At the west end there were extensive carriage sidings in the centre of the triangle formed by the lines to Halifax and Cleckheaton. Passenger services on the Cleckheaton line ceased in June 1965, but the line remained open for freight and specials until 1981. Fowler 2-6-4T No 42406 sets off from the station, which is behind the bridge in the top left-hand side, with an evening stopping train from Bradford to Penistone.

Now: 2 November 1994
Any sign of Low Moor being a big and busy railway junction, which it was 30 years ago, have completely vanished. The site of the old carriage sidings lay derelict for many years, but is currently being developed as an industrial estate. West Yorkshire PTE Class 158 No 158902 passes with the 13.19 York-Manchester Victoria train.
Author (2)

Halifax Town station

Then: 17 August 1959

At this time the unique Stanier Class 5 No 44767 was a frequent performer on the Bradford-Liverpool Exchange expresses. The two portions of the train, from Bradford Exchange and Leeds Central, will have been joined at Low Moor or, possibly, at Halifax. This is the ex-L&YR part of the station; to the left were the ex-Great Northern platforms (to serve the lines to Bradford and Keighley via Queensbury). In the background is Beacon Hill and the once famous Macintosh toffee factory.

Now: 1 November 1994

The station name has varied over the years, but is now plain 'Halifax'. Today only one island platform is in use on the former LMS side. It is not possible to copy the original picture exactly, but this is as near as I could manage. The view is partly obscured by one of the buildings constructed in connection with the 'Eureka' museum, which is a 'hands on' museum for children and has been much encouraged by Prince Charles. The old goods yards are now occupied by this project. Unit No 158767 is shown leaving with the 12.53 train from Selby to Manchester Victoria.

Author (2)

Halifax (west end)

Then: 15 July 1959
The unique Stanier Class 5, with Stephenson Link motion, No 44767, then allocated to Bank Hall, makes a fine sight as it leaves with an evening express to Liverpool. The start of the marshalling yard, which continued behind the station to the far end, can be seen on the left hand side.
Now: 1 November 1994
All that remains at Halifax other than the one island platform is one siding for stabling DMUs on a shuttle service from Bradford. As can be seen the track now runs through a small avenue of trees, not one of which appeared to be present in 1959. Beacon Hill is seen in the background, the railway passing through it in a 1,105yd-long tunnel. Class 158 No 158781 leaves on the 13.19 York-Manchester Victoria service.
Author (2)

Ripponden

Then: Unknown

The 3¾ mile branch from Sowerby Bridge to Rishworth opened in 1878 to Ripponden and to Rishworth in 1881. It was closed to passengers on 21 September 1929 (due to tramway competition) at which time the service was operated by one of the Hughes railmotors. The line remained open for freight until 30 August 1958 and was eventually lifted in 1962.

Now: 23 December 1994

Today the site has become a housing estate, although behind the houses a retaining wall can still be seen and the bridge abutments which supported the bridge over the road are still clearly visible.

Ian Allan Library/Author

Sowerby Bridge (east)

Then: 10 August 1958

The railway arrived in 1849, but the original station was replaced in 1876. The branch to Ripponden opened in 1878 and was extended to Rishworth three years later. Normally worked in its later years by one of the Hughes-designed ex-L&YR railmotors, the branch lost its passenger service in July 1929. The branch joined the main line from the left of the picture from under Scar Head Hill.

The woollen industry of the area is much in evidence as local 'WD' 2-8-0 No 90650 leaves with a second portion of a train that had split in the station and heads towards Wakefield.

Now: 16 November 1994

The bay platforms at the station have long since gone, as have all the sidings; there are now only the two through lines. There is a very frequent service to Manchester Victoria and Blackpool in the west and to Bradford and further east in the other direction. Class 158 No 158774 passes non-stop on the 12.47 from Blackpool to York.

The undergrowth has taken over the original tracks, and a small factory has been built over the Rishworth branch. Some high-rise flats have appeared on the skyline.

Author (2)

Sowerby Bridge (west)

Then: 15 March 1959

This superb panoramic view is taken from above the east entrance to Sowerby Bridge tunnel. On the horizon can be seen Wainhouse Tower, a splendid structure of no practical use whatsoever, other, than it is said, for a wealthy businessman to be able to look over a high wall into his neighbour's garden. On the right is the West signalbox, which controlled the up loop and yard, whilst on the left is the locomotive depot (originally 25E and later 56E). The depot retained an L&Y atmosphere to the late 1950s, with an allocation of 0-6-0s. It provided motive power for local passenger duties, but was mainly a freight shed especially for Mytholmroyd yard about three miles to the west. A new roof and lighting were installed around 1955, but the depot closed in January 1964.

Now: 1 November 1994

Wainhouse Folly still stands on the horizon, but the shed, signalbox and yards have completely vanished; the box was ultimately burnt down by local vandals (a fate that also befell the superb mock-Gothic station building). The shed site is now used by a haulage contractor, and the Class 158s and Sprinters glide silently by several times per hour, a ritual that is interspersed with the occasional freight normally headed by a Class 56 or 60. Unit No 158777 heads west on the 13.46 York-Blackpool train.

Author (2)

Hebden Bridge (east)

Then: 27 February 1960
The station can just be seen in the distance, as Bank Hall 'Jubilee' No 45698 *Mars* heads towards York on the 10.30am Liverpool Exchange-Newcastle train. This was the only Liverpool-Newcastle train of the day to use the Calder Valley route, and the Bank Hall (27A) trio of 'Jubilees' — *Mars*, *Dauntless* and *Glorious* — worked the train for many years.

Now: 14 December 1994
Since the lifting of the up and down loops between Mytholmroyd and Hebden Bridge the trees have grown very quickly. West Yorkshire PTE Class 158 No 158904, on the 12.47 Manchester Victoria-Selby service, passes through what is now an avenue of trees.
Author (2)

Hebden Bridge station

Then: Unknown
Now: 14 December 1994
The station opened on 5 October 1840 and, as can be seen, the platforms were staggered. Little has changed over the years except the signalling and the goods yard on the left has become the car park. The station is extremely well maintained retaining much of its traditional atmosphere — note the signs on the westbound platform. The 13.47 from Manchester Victoria to York, comprised of Class 158 No 158781, is shown ready to depart.
Ian Allan Library/Author

Hall Royd Junction

Then: 14 June 1961
At this time the triangle around Todmorden/Stansfield Hall Junction/Hall Royd Junction — was still fully in use. This continued until March 1973 when the Todmorden-Stansfield Hall line was taken out of use. As can be seen there were extensive sidings within the triangle. The banking locomotives used to wait by the concrete hut in the background, and this duty represented one of the last steam turns on BR. 'WD' 2-8-0 No 90523 pauses in the down loop with an empty coal train, returning to one of the Yorkshire pits. There were signalboxes at each corner of the triangle.

Now: 1 November 1994
The tracks into the centre of the triangle remain (just), but appear to have vanished beneath the undergrowth. All the loops have been lifted. After a period of freight only use, the Hall Royd Junction-Burnley line saw a passenger service (initially sponsored by a building society) reintroduced in the early 1980s. A West Yorkshire PTE Class 158 No 158909 heads towards Hebden Bridge on the 09.45 service from Manchester Victoria to York.
Author (2)

Walsden

Then: 10 June 1968
The evening sunshine catches Stanier '8F' No 48356 as it climbs towards Summit Tunnel with a loaded coal train past the site of the present Walsden station. The former station (which closed on 7 August 1961) was behind the photographer, the platforms starting immediately after the 306yd-long Winterbutlee Tunnel.

Now: 14 December 1994
The 12.24 York-Manchester train, formed of Class 158 No 158905, pauses at the new station at Walsden. The road, railway and canal all fit into the narrow valley towards Todmorden.
Author (2)

Smithy Bridge

Then: 5 April 1959
The original station opened in October 1868. This view is looking eastwards towards Todmorden and, as can be seen, the platforms were staggered either side of the level crossing.
Now: 23 December 1994
Following closure on 1 May 1960 the platforms that served the original station were demolished. When the station was reopened in August 1985 the opportunity was taken to resite the eastbound platform on the Manchester side of the crossing. West Yorkshire PTE Class 158/9 No 158903 is pictured leaving the station and passing the site of the old station on the 11.47 Manchester-York service. The attractive ex-L&YR box remains largely unchanged.
Author (2)

Rochdale

Then: 19 August 1961
This important station was opened in July 1839 and was later to become a junction for the lines to Bacup (now closed) and Oldham (which survives). Stanier 2-6-0 No 42945, which was the first of the class, arrives with the 11.47am Bolton (Trinity Street)-Leeds train. The photograph is taken at the west end of the station looking towards Manchester.

Now: 23 December 1994
The platform on the right of the 'Then' photograph remains in use after the extensive rationalisation and rebuilding of the station. The platform from which the earlier photograph was taken is now out of use and all the land to the left, which used to house bay platforms and other through platforms, is now derelict.

West Yorkshire PTE No 158910 arrives at the station with the 12.47 from Manchester Victoria to Selby.
Author (2)

Cheetham Hill (Manchester)

Then: 2 June 1968
The last operational 'Britannia' class Pacific, No 70013 *Oliver Cromwell*, working one of the many specials at the end of main line steam on British Rail, is pictured hauling the empty stock for a special out of the extensive carriage sidings to the east of Manchester Victoria. The sidings were situated about ¾-mile out of Victoria on the loop line to Thorpes Bridge Junction.

Now: 29 December 1994
As can be seen, virtually all the tracks have been lifted and the area is now empty and derelict — a victim of the decline of BR's locomotive-hauled carriage fleet. It is to be wondered why two merry-go-round wagons have been left dumped off the end of the track.
Author (2)

Manchester Victoria

Then: Mid-1960s

This is the old familiar scene which greeted passengers over the years — the steam bankers for Miles Platting Bank simmering gently as they waited their next duty, whilst a Metro-Cammell Class 101 DMU heads for Exchange station from Leeds and a Calder Valley Class 110 unit waits to head west. The Stanier Class 5 is No 44938, and behind it is a 2-6-4T.

Now: 11 December 1994

The contrast between old and new could not be greater. The old station has been modernised and rationalised. A diverted trans-Pennine working, which had travelled via the Calder Valley route rather than over Standedge, prepares to leave for Liverpool from the new Platform 3.

Colin T. Gifford/Author

Manchester Victoria (west end)

Then: 4 August 1968
Opened in 1844 Victoria provided both through and terminus platforms. Stanier Class 5 No 45156, formerly called *Ayrshire Yeomanry*, is pictured halfway down the connecting platform between Victoria and Exchange stations — a platform which was the longest in Britain. The locomotive is heading one of the steam specials that ran on the last weekend of regular steam operation on BR.

Now: 11 December 1994
The changes wrought during 1993 and 1994 to the station have been dramatic and are currently not yet finished. Fortunately, the fine facade, which used to house the headquarters of the L&YR, have been retained. Since nationalisation Victoria has tended to play second fiddle to Piccadilly which, with electrification, has had considerable sums spent upon it over the years. However, it appears that Victoria is now catching up with the latest developments. The number of platforms has been gradually reduced and some of the bay platforms, which used to serve the local services to the north and east, have been taken over by the new Metrolink system. Today construction continues above the new station platforms and the running lines have been moved over to avoid the site of the now-closed Exchange. The attractive facade of the old station can be seen on the extreme right. Above the station is being built a new sports stadium.
Author (2)

Miles Platting Junction

Then: Mid-1950s
Situated at the top of the 1 in 47/59 gradient from Manchester Victoria, this was the point where the direct line from Victoria to Thorpes Bridge Junction parted from the LNW line over Standedge. In days of steam most of the expresses were double-headed, and other trains banked up the gradient. A Liverpool-Newcastle express headed by two Farnley Junction (Leeds) locomotives — 'Jubilee' No 45646 *Napier* and Class 5 No 45080 — round the sharp curve heading east.

Now: 11 December 1994
The station originally opened in 1844 and is currently still open although the state of the platforms would suggest otherwise as Greater Manchester PTE-liveried Class 142 No 142013 passes with a special working to Stalybridge. At the moment Miles Platting station is the subject of possible closure proposals.
K. Field/Author

Ashton Moss North Junction

Then: Mid-1950s
An unrebuilt 'Patriot' No 45515 *Caernarvon* passes the junction heading the 3.15pm slow train from Manchester to Leeds. The electrified line coming in at the junction represented a link to the exchange sidings at this point from the electrified ex-Great Central line over Woodhead to Sheffield.

Now: 26 November 1994
It is surprising how little has changed at this location over the 40 years since the 'Then' photograph. There has been some rationalisation of track and, although the masts still stand, the 1,500V dc overhead has been removed. The signalbox and most of the semaphore signals, however, remain, as Pacer No 142036 heads towards Manchester with the 13.25 service from Wakefield.
K. Field/Author

Droylsden

Then: 1950s
Droylsden station station opened in 1846 and formed the junction for the ex-LNWR line towards Stockport. Stanier Class 5 No 45077 passes through the station with a Colne-Stockport service. By the time of this photograph the Stockport line platforms were no longer in use and the buildings were being demolished.

Now: 26 November 1994
The local pub in the background provides a reference point but, apart from that, little remains other than the double track of the Manchester-Huddersfield line over which Class 150/1 No 150140 passes on the 13.55 Manchester-Wakefield service. Droyslden station was closed finally on 7 October 1968 and the ex-LNWR route succumbed on 6 July 1969.
K. Field/Author

Queens Road (Manchester)

Then: 16 April 1976
One of the Class 504 EMUs built for the Bury electrified lines at Wolverton in 1954 is shown passing Queens Road signalbox *en route* for Manchester. The train is painted in Greater Manchester PTE livery. These units continued in service until the summer of 1991 when services over the Bury line were suspended as it was rebuilt for use by the new Metrolink system.

Now: 29 December 1994
One of Metrolink's 26 Italian-built articulated trams heads towards Manchester past the site of Queens Road box. The tracks on the left head for the Metrolink depot.
Author (2)

Bury Knowsley Street

Then: 2 March 1963
Caprotti Stanier Class 5 No 44743 enters the station whilst working the 8.14am service from Southport to Rochdale. The steep dip in the track that can be seen was known as the 'Bury Hollow', which allowed the line to pass under the route to Bolton Street station (on which a Class 504 EMU can just be seen). The spur up to Bolton Street climbed so steeply that the up line, on which the train is show, is higher than the down line.

Now: 29 December 1994
In order to show how the old line has been completely filled in the 'Now' picture is taken from a slightly higher angle. Stock from the preserved East Lancs Railway can just be seen and the newly-laid track on the right represents the ELR's extension to Heywood. Knowsley Street closed on 5 October 1970.
R. S. Greenwood/Author

Bury South Signalbox

Then: 2 November 1974
A photograph taken from the end of the platform at Bury Bolton Street station looking southwards shows a Class 504 EMU passing the signalbox as it arrives on the 08.30 working from Manchester Victoria.

Now: 29 December 1994
As with the previous 'Now' shot, this too has been taken from a higher angle in order to illustrate better the current layout. A Class 08 shunter of the East Lancs Railway is parked on the track to Heywood, which crosses the new tramway just around the corner (out of sight on the left). Coaching stock is stored on the right-hand line, whilst the other line goes to the former depot, situated beyond the now-closed footbridge, which is the main engineering centre for the preserved line. BR services into Bolton Street were withdrawn on 17 March 1980, when trains were diverted into a new station.
D. A. Flitcroft/Author

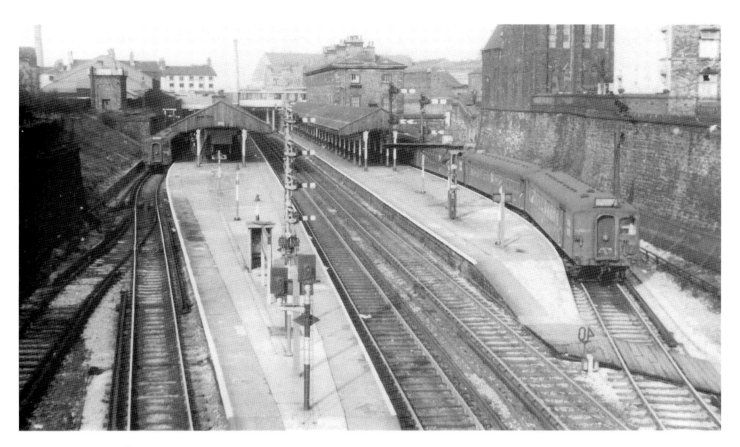

Bury Bolton Street

Then: 27 March 1959
The station opened in 1846 and served trains between Manchester and Rawtenstall or Accrington. It was also the junction station for the short branch to Holcombe Brook. Passenger services north of Bolton Street succumbed from Stubbins Junction to Accrington on 5 December 1966 and from Bury to Rawtenstall on 2 June 1972. Coal trains continued to serve the line to Rawtenstall until April 1981. The service from Bolton Street south to Manchester (along with the branch to Holcombe Book) were electrified by the L&YR and two of the five-car sets built from 1916 at Newton Heath are shown in the platforms.

Now: 11 December 1994
As a result of the dedication and determination of a band of enthusiasts over many years, the station eventually became the home of the East Lancashire Railway. With considerable support from the various local authorities the line northwards was progressively reopened, until, on 27 April 1991, the first through train ran to Rawtenstall. Since then progress has been very rapid, making the ELR one of the most important preserved railways in the country.

Comparison between the two pictures show that very little has changed to the railway layout, although the station buildings and surrounding structures have altered considerably. There is also the provision of a new car park.
R. J. Farrell/Author

Heywood

Then: 1 November 1959
'Jubilee' class No 45653 *Barham* storms away from Heywood, situated on the Bury Knowsley Street-Castleton line, after an unaided climb of the 1 in 85 Broadfield Bank, with 10 coaches, on a Blackpool-Doncaster excursion.

Holcombe Brook

Then: 1952
The short but steeply graded branch, which was just over three miles in length, had a very interesting history. Opened in 1882 it was steam operated until electrification in July 1913. Initially it was electrified with a 3,500V dc overhead system that had been provided at the expense of Dick Kerr & Co of Preston (a company later to form part of English Electric and GEC). The company wanted a line on which it could test the system prior to trying to obtain business in Brazil. As a result the steam railmotor service was replaced on 29 July 1913. The rolling stock, built by the L&YR, was similar to that which later operated in Liverpool. Following the conversion of the

Heap Bridge Junction

Then: 15 September 1964
The route from Rochdale westwards through
Bury and on to Bolton formed part of a
cross-country link with Liverpool. The
section from Heywood to Bury opened on
1 May 1848. Heap Bridge Junction was
situated just east of Bury Knowsley Street on
Broadfield Bank. From the junction a short
freight-only branch served Heap Bridge.
Class 5 No 44733 is caught storming up the
bank with a Blackpool-Failsworth relief
train.
Now: 23 December 1994
After the closure of the Bury-Rochdale line
to passenger services on 5 October 1970 it
remained open for freight until 1981,
although the branch to Heap Bridge was
finally closed in December 1973. Reflecting
the decline in the region's industrial base,
the number of mill chimneys visible has
declined, although it will not be long before
steam returns to the now disused line as the
formation forms part of the East Lancashire
Railway's extension to Heywood.
I. G. Holt/Author

Now: 23 December 1994
The station closed to passenger services on
5 October 1970. The line from Castleton
remained open until 1981 to provide access
for freight trains to serve Rawtenstall. Since
that date the route has been truncated to
serve a wagon works at Heywood. Little
remains from the earlier view today,
although the track on the left is still available
and will eventually form part of an extension
to the East Lancashire Railway.
R. S. Greenwood/Author

Manchester-Bury line to 1,200V dc third-rail
operation, the Holcombe Brook route was
reconverted in March 1918. Third-rail
services continued until 1951 when steam
was reintroduced. Steam reigned supreme
until the line's closure on 4 May 1952 as
shown in this wintry scene — note the
remains of the third-rail.
Now: 3 December
Freight continued to serve Holcombe Brook
until June 1960, but today you would be hard
pressed to realise that the town possessed a
railway. The site of the station is now a
shopping centre.
Ian Allan Library/Author

Colne

Then: 2 August 1968
The first railway to reach Colne was the Midland Railway branch from Skipton via Earby, which opened to all traffic on 2 October 1848. At Colne this line made a head-on junction with the East Lancashire Railway's line from Burnley which opened for all traffic on 1 February the following year. This then provided a further trans-Pennine route.

During the last few days of steam operation on British Railways, Class 5 No 45407 of Lostock Hall prepares to leave the yard at Colne with the evening van train to Preston.

Now: 3 December 1994
The line north from Colne to Skipton was closed to passenger services on 2 February 1970 and the track subsequently lifted, thus making Colne a terminus for a branch running southwestwards. The site of the original station was demolished and landscaped and the town is now served by a single-track line provided with bus shelter buildings. The Class 5 is happily now preserved and has been very active on the main line in recent years, including the West Highland route between Mallaig and Fort William.
Author (2)

Rose Grove

Then: 27 April 1968
One of the many specials run in the area during the last months of steam operation over BR pauses for water alongside Rose Grove West signalbox. Standard Class 5s Nos 73050 and 73069, from Patricroft shed, provide the motive power. Rose Grove was once an important centre, with lines radiating to Skipton, Padiham, Todmorden and Accrington. There was also the steam depot, visible to the left, with its coaling stage hidden by the exhaust. The railway first reached the town in 1848 and the shed was opened in 1899. Rose Grove shed survived to be one of the last BR steam depots, finally closing on 5 August 1968.

Now: 3 December 1994
Trees prevent the photographer from standing in exactly the same spot and the M65 motorway now passes through the site of the shed behind the trees on the left as Class 158 No 158805 forms the 14.18 Leeds-Blackpool North service. The station is still open and is situated behind the bridge in the background. No 73050 also survives and is now preserved on the Nene Valley Railway.
Author (2)

Huncoat

Now: 1 June 1968
The station is situated between Accrington and Rose Grove and was opened on 18 June 1848. During the last few weeks of steam on BR the Saturdays Only afternoon Colne-Red Bank van train received much attention from enthusiasts. The foreman at Rose Grove had been persuaded on this occasion to roster '8F' 2-8-0 No 48257 rather than the usual Class 5 for the duty, and some hasty cleaning of the smokebox and buffer beam was carried out before departure. It is seen passing the station.

Now: 3 December 1994
The station, served by the service to Colne, is still open, although as can be seen the original buildings have been demolished. An unidentified Class 158 passes non-stop on the 13.47 from Blackpool North to Leeds. Behind the photographer is a level crossing which is still controlled by a fine signalbox.

Author (2)

Accrington

Then: 2 August 1968
Railways reached the town on 19 June 1848 when the line from Blackburn was opened. This was followed on 17 August 1848 with the opening of the line from Stubbins Junction (Ramsbottom). Services were extended to Burnley on 18 September the following year. The evening Colne-Preston van train takes the line towards Stubbins Junction hauled by Class 5 No 45407. Passenger and freight services over the Stubbins Junction line had been withdrawn on 5 December 1966. The train used the platform to load parcels before reversing back out on to the main line to continue to Blackburn and Preston. It has just passed over the fine viaduct across the town.
Now: 3 December 1994
All traces of the Stubbins Junction line have now been removed. A West Yorkshire PTE Class 158 No 158902 makes a very cautious approach over the sharp curve into the station on the 13.18 Leeds-Blackpool North service. In the background is the viaduct which has recently been cleaned. *Author (2)*

Wilpshire

Then: Undated
The station is situated on the
Blackburn-Hellifield line, which
was opened as far as Clitheroe in
1850 and throughout in 1880. As
can be seen the station nameboard
reads 'Wilpshire for Ribchester'.
Then: 20 April 1968
The station at Wilpshire lost is
passenger service on 10 September
1962 and freight facilities were
withdrawn in November 1964. The
line, however, remained open and
was used by many of the last BR
steam specials in 1968 and here
two Stanier Class 5s, Nos 45342
and 45156, are shown heading
south towards Blackburn.
Now: 6 January 1995
Although local passenger services
over the line disappeared in 1962,
the line was retained for freight, for
diversionary use from the West
Coast main line and latterly for
steam specials. Amongst the
heaviest users of the line were,
until recently, the cement trains
from Clitheroe. Following pressure
from a local group passenger
services were reinstated between
Blackburn and Clitheroe on
30 May 1994 and the hourly
service now runs through to Shaw
(on the Oldham line). A Class 150
No 150215 passes the site of the
old station (the buildings of which
still stand as a house) *en route* to
Shaw. *Ian Allan Library/Author (2)*

Clitheroe

Then: Undated
The railway to Clitheroe opened to the public on 22 June 1850 at which stage the line was completed through to Chatburn (one station north of Clitheroe) along with the Horrocksford branch.

Now: 6 January 1995
Passenger services over the line were withdrawn in September 1962 although the line remained open for freight (largely the cement traffic from Horrocksford) and as a diversionary route. Passenger services south from Clitheroe were restored on 30 May 1994 as the result of hard and patient work by a local group. Class 150/2 No 150215 is pictured leaving the newly-constructed station on the 15.55 service to Shaw.
Ian Allan Library/Author

Gisburn Tunnel

Then: 28 July 1968
The Chatburn-Gisburn section of the line was opened to all traffic on 2 June 1879 and the final section to Hellifield, the most northerly point reached by the L&YR, followed on 1 June 1880. Although closed to regular passenger services in 1962, the route was used by many of the final steam specials in 1968. The last 'Britannia' in service, No 70013 *Oliver Cromwell*, was a frequent performer on these trains and is pictured emerging from the 176yd-long tunnel. It will be noted that the tunnel possesses extremely ornate portals.

Now: 24 April 1993
Following the cessation of freight traffic the line survives only for diversionary use and for the occasional steam special, although there are hopes that the service to Clitheroe will be extended northwards to Hellifield. A diverted train, the down 'Royal Scot', leaves the tunnel with super power in the form of Class 60 No 60094 *Tryfan*, piloting Class 47 No 47973 *Derby Evening Telegraph*.
Author (2)

Bamber Bridge

Then: May 1957
The Preston-Blackburn line opened in 1846, Bamber Bridge station being situated on the outskirts of Preston.
Now: 6 January 1995
Surprisingly, over a period of 37 years the station retains some of the features from the 'Then' illustration, particularly the distinctive signalbox that controls the level crossing. The station has recently been tidied up as is shown in the picture of Class 158 No 158760 heading east on the 12.47 Blackpool North-York train. There is an attractive pub situated by the crossing named 'The Lancashire & Yorkshire'.
T. Lewis/Author

Preston

Then: 15 January 1968
The East Lancashire Railway eventually opened its own direct line from Bamber Bridge to Preston in 1850 and further extensions to the station were completed in 1913. Class 5 No 45397 is seen passing through the station with a rake of empty wagons heading towards Todd Lane.

Now: 6 January 1995
The railways ceased to use the tracks occupied by No 45397 in 1972 when the section from Preston No 4 to Preston East Lancs Junction was taken out of service. Over the past 20 years the site has been transformed to provide a large car park. In the background the remaining station continues in operation.
C. Foss/Author

Lostock Hall Junction

Then: 19 July 1968
Class 5 No 45287 heads through the junction, situated to the south of Preston, with a freight. This must have been one of the last duties for the locomotive as its shed closed within a month. Visible on the skyline is the coaling stage for Lostock Hall shed.

Now: 5 February 1994
It is still easy to see that these two pictures are at the same location, but nearly everything has changed. All the shunting yards have gone, the coaling stage has been demolished, the station moved from the west side to the east side of the bridge and the electrification masts have appeared.

The occasion of the second photograph was a special Class 50 railtour, the 'Midland Scotsman', for which the two locomotives were painted into their original blue livery, without names, just as they had worked the West Coast main line. Nos D433 and D400 leave the junction and head towards Blackburn and the Settle-Carlisle line for Beattock and Glasgow. The train returned southwards over the West Coast route.
S. S. Hancock/Author

Lostock Hall Shed

Then: 4 August 1968
Lostock Hall was the shed that served all L&YR operations in the Preston area. It was originally opened in 1882 and had an allocation of some 60 locomotives. Its final shed code, from 1963, was 10D; before that date it was 24C. The night shot was taken on the day before closure (5 August 1968) and the well-cleaned locomotives which were in steam were ready for the steam specials the following morning. Stanier Class 5 No 44894 awaits its last duty.
Now: 6 January 1995
Following closure the site has been cleared and is currently derelict; it is still possible, however, to trace where the running lines used to be
Author (2)

Lostock Hall

Then: 22 August 1966
Stanier Class 5 No 45326 blows off as it slows for a stop at the station. At this date the station was situated on the other side of the road bridge from which this photograph was taken.

Now: 6 January 1995
The original station closed on 6 October 1969. It was, however, reopened on 14 May 1984 on this side of the bridge. Class 158 No 158763 is shown passing the station on the 11.46 from York to Blackpool North. Ironically the eastbound platform stands in the place of the now-demolished Lostock Hall Station signalbox.
A. W. Hobson/Author

Blackpool North

Then: 11 April 1966
All the lines on the Fylde peninsula — those to Fleetwood, Blackpool North and Blackpool Central — were jointly owned by the L&YR and the LNWR. With the famous tower, opened in 1895, in the background there is plenty of action on this Easter Monday in the station. There are five excursion trains, all steam hauled, in the platforms.

Now: 6 January 1995
The station was completely reconstructed during 1973 and 1974 when many of the platforms were taken out of service. In contrast to the busy Easter illustrated in the 'Then' shot, this January Friday saw only one Class 158 and one Class 156 present and both of these quickly departed on their return journeys. The signals still remain, although reduced in number, and all the sidings around the station have gone. Currently in store in sidings about half a mile from the station are withdrawn EMUs and DMUs. Through services from London Euston have now been abandoned by InterCity.
W. D. Ballard/Author

St Annes

Then: 8 April 1966
Construction of the Blackpool & Lytham Railway started in 1861 and the line was opened on 6 April 1863. Originally known as Cross Slack, the station was renamed Lytham in 1875. The surprise closure of Blackpool Central station came in November 1964, following the withdrawal of services over the direct Blackpool South-Kirkham line in the previous September. Not long before the reorganisation, the 6.30pm Blackpool Central-Manchester service calls at St Annes headed by 'Clan' class Pacific No 72006 *Clan MacKenzie*.

Now: 6 January 1995
Following the closure to Central, the line to Blackpool South was retained, but reduced to a single line, effectively becoming no more than a long siding from Kirkham. The new buildings are neat and tidy, but are in sharp contrast to the past. They are, however, adequate to cater for the single Class 153 unit No 153363 which is working the 09.16 service from Colne to the new Blackpool South station.
C. Spring/Author

Agecroft Junction

Then: August 1967
The railway reached Agecroft, situated between Salford and Bolton, very early, with the line of the Manchester, Bolton & Bury Canal Navigation Railway opening on 29 May 1838. Although there was originally a station on the site, this was closed as early as 1861. Agecroft Junction connected the original 1838 line with Brindle Heath Junction, which is on the line between Pendlebury and Walkden. Agecroft shed was opened in 1888 to house 48 locomotives, covering both passenger and freight turns. The shed was closed in 1966 and subsequently demolished. Class 5 No 44800 heads towards Manchester with a parcels train.
Now: 18 June 1992
There has been some track rationalisation, but the line between Bolton and Manchester is still operational. InterCity-liveried Class 47 No 47808 is seen passing the junction whilst working the 12.45 Glasgow-Paddington service. The site of the shed remains derelict, whilst the background is dominated by the power station, which has recently been demolished.
Ian Krause/Author

Bolton (east)

Then: Undated
Stanier 2-6-4T No 42444 is pictured approaching Bolton station at Bolton East Junction with a train that appears to have come off the line from Bury. This route can be seen heading off behind the signalbox.

Now: 29 December 1994
The extensive goods yards have all gone, as have the signals and signalbox. The overgrown sidings on the right were used for parcels traffic until the services were withdrawn on 1 October 1993. Sprinter No 150205 is pictured heading for Manchester. The floodlights of Bolton Wanderers' football ground, Burnden Park, can be seen on the left in both pictures. Passenger services on the line between Bolton, Bury and Rochdale were withdrawn on 5 October 1970 and freight services over the route as far as Bury succumbed on the same date.
C. B. Golding/Author

Bolton Station

Then: Undated
Unfortunately, the photograph is undated, but it shows the complex of lines that served Bolton station before rationalisation. Bolton was at the hub of a network of ex-L&YR lines that served Blackburn, Preston, Manchester and Bury, being first connected to the railway system in 1838. A separate station served the ex-LNWR lines, all of which have now closed. With the exception of the Bury line, closed in 1970, Bolton retains its ex-L&YR routes.

Now: 29 December 1994
Comparison between the two photographs illustrates clearly the considerable changes that have occurred over the past decades. The only common features seem to be the town hall clock tower and the roof over the up platform. Class 47 No 47851 leaves the station heading the up 'Sussex Scot', the 10.40 Glasgow Central-Brighton service.
Real Photos/Author

Horwich

Then: 23 June 1953

This short branch, which left the main Bolton-Preston line at Blackrod, was opened for freight services on 15 July 1868 and to passenger trains on 14 February 1870. More than a decade later Horwich was to be selected as the site of the L&YR's new Locomotive Works; the first locomotives were constructed at the works in 1888 and the now-preserved No 1008 was the first completed locomotive to emerge in February 1889. One of the ex-L&YR 2-4-2Ts, No 50646, is shown about to depart with a passenger service to Blackrod.

Now: 29 December 1994

Passenger services over the branch were withdrawn on 27 September 1965 and normal freight facilities ceased a year later. The branch, however, survive to serve the foundry at Horwich, the only part of the former works to remain operational. The site of the station has now been redeveloped into a pleasant park with sports facilities; the wheels, mounted on a plinth, stand to remind locals of the area's history.

N. R. Knight/Author

Ormskirk

Then: 5 November 1960

The line from Walton Junction (Liverpool) to Lostock Hall Junction (Preston) opened throughout on 2 April 1849. Amongst the intermediate stations served was Ormskirk, and Stanier 2-6-4T No 42433 is pictured ready to leave northbound on the 3.36pm service to Southport.

Now: 31 December 1994

Ormskirk is now the terminus for the Merseyrail third-rail electrified service from Liverpool and the track in the one remaining operational platform has been split physically. North of Ormskirk services are operated to Preston using Pacer units and through passengers have to change at this station. The track on the right remains extant, although unused, for emergency purposes. Note that the brickwork from the now-demolished signalbox survives as Class 507 No 507016 is ready to depart for Liverpool on the far side of the 'great divide'.

L. Sandler/Author

Hoddlesden Junction

Then: 1 June 1968
The junction is situated on the steeply-graded line from Bolton to Blackburn, between Darwen and Spring Vale. The line between Blackburn and Bolton opened in stages during 1847 and 1848. The junction was for the freight-only branch to Hoddlesden, which closed in 1950. Lower Darwen shed was about 1½ miles from the junction in the Blackburn direction. It opened in 1881 and closed in February 1966. Class 8F No 48257 passes the signalbox heading the Colne-Red Bank vans train. The lines on the left remained at this date to serve a local paper mill.
Now: 3 December 1994
Everything is now lifted with the exception of the single line which carries the Bolton-Blackburn service. Class 150/1 No 150135, in the Greater Manchester Council livery, passes *en route* to Clitheroe.
Author (2)

Southport Chapel Street

Then: 24 August 1971

The railway arrived at Chapel Street through an extension of the Liverpool, Crosby & Southport Railway on 22 August 1851. This was not the only terminus to serve Southport, as the Cheshire Lines Committee operated into the now-closed Lord Street and there was also a freight terminus at Kensington Road. The station seems remarkably empty for 1971 with only two of the old Class 502 EMU sets, built at Derby between 1939 and 1941, visible. The photograph was taken from the signalbox.

Now: 31 December 1994

The signalbox has now been demolished as a result of the recently completed modernisation of the signalling on Merseyrail. Many of the carriage sidings have now vanished as the vast influx of specials in the summer months are something of the past. The platforms on the extreme right have now become the inevitable car park. Pacer unit No 142042 is shown arriving with a working that had originated at Chester.

R. E. Ruffell/Author

Bank Hall

Then: 14 October 1951
Class 502 EMU No M28311 presents a
rather depressing sight as it enters Bank Hall
station, Liverpool, on a train from Southport.
The line from Southport to Waterloo,
originally built by the Liverpool, Crosby &
Southport Railway, opened on 24 July 1848
and was extended in September 1850.
Acquired by the L&YR in 1855, by the early
years of the 20th century there were more
than 80 trains per day in each direction.
Electric services between Liverpool
Exchange and Southport were introduced on
22 March 1904.
Now: 31 December 1994
Today things have been brightened up a little
and much to the author's surprise one of
Merseyrail's deicing units, formed of ex-
Class 501 stock, turned up rather than the
Class 507 or 508 units which normally
monopolise the services over the line.
K. Field/Author

Walton (Liverpool)

Then: 12 May 1965
In the days when there was a through service
from Preston to Liverpool Exchange over
this route, Standard Class 4MT No 75026,
fitted with a double chimney, enters the
station with the 2.55pm service from
Preston.
Now: 31 December 1994
Although the over bridge in the distance
remains unchanged, elsewhere much has
altered over the past three decades. The
station buildings have been demolished and
improved lighting has been provided.
Class 507 No 507016, painted in the
attractive yellow livery of Merseyrail,
departs from the station with a service to
Ormskirk. On the far left can be seen the
walls of Walton Jail.
I. G. Holt/Author

Liverpool Exchange

Then: 5 August 1963

Liverpool Exchange was to become the L&YR's terminus in the city. Originally the L&YR was served by a station at Tithebarn Street, but with the expansion of services the facilities at this station proved inadequate. Plans were first developed in the mid-1870s for the construction of a new station — effectively an enlargement of the first station — and the first platforms at Exchange were brought into service on 12 December 1886. The station served trains for Manchester and beyond, as well as the suburban routes. It was provided with 10 platforms. From one of these Stanier 2-6-4T No 42550 is pictured ready to depart on the 3pm service to Bolton.

Now: 31 December 1994

Following rationalisation and the transfer of the remaining services away from the station, Exchange was finally closed on 30 April 1977. The site has been subsequently cleared and has become the inevitable car park. It is possible, however, still to trace the location of the platforms, but apart from that all else has been swept away. *D. A. Idle/Author*

Wigan Wallgate

Then: Undated
This picture was probably taken in the late 1950s as the locomotive is carrying a 27C shedplate for Southport, which received five of these locomotives when new! Standard Class 4MT No 75016 is shown drifting down the bank into the station on a train from Manchester to Southport.
Now: 31 December 1994
The background has changed completely and the overhead catenary masts of the West Coast main line can be seen alongside as a Pacer in Merseyrail livery, No 142056, leaves on the 14.02 service from Southport to Stockport.
J. Davenport/Author

North Staffordshire Railway

The North Staffordshire Railway, the 'Knotty', was one of the smaller railways to form part of the LMS at the Grouping in 1923; none the less it was an important operator within the Potteries and, to this day, many of the routes that the railway built remain essential links.

The North Staffordshire Railway was authorised by Parliament in 1846 to construct a network of lines to the east of Stoke-on-Trent. The first section to be completed, that between Norton Bridge and Stoke itself, was opened on 17 April 1848. This was quickly followed by further openings — between Stoke and Uttoxeter on 7 August 1848, between Stoke and Crewe and Congleton and Harecastle on 9 October 1848, between Stone and Colwich on 1 May 1849, between Congleton and Macclesfield on 13 June 1849 and between North Rode and Uttoxeter (via the Churnet Valley) on 13 July 1849.

The stimulus for the development of the railway's network came from both the Staffordshire coal field and from the numerous pottery works that gave the district its popular name. Thus, through the 19th century the railway continued to expand culminating in the early years of the 20th century with the opening of the branch to Cheadle in 1901 and the construction of the narrow gauge Leek & Manifold Railway which opened in 1904. The final extension, that to Trentham Park, was opened in 1910.

At the Grouping, the LMS inherited a compact network of lines and more than 200 standard gauge locomotives. In addition, three steam rail motors and two narrow gauge engines also passed to the LMS. In terms of motive power, the NSR was the sixth largest of the pre-Grouping constituents of the LMS.

The LMS years saw the first significant contractions in the ex-NSR network with the closure in 1927 of the branch to Biddulph to passenger services. This was followed in 1930 by the closure of the Sandbach branch to passenger services. A similar fate befell the Audley line in 1931. Three years later the narrow gauge Leek & Manifold Railway closed completely. The final closure in the interwar years saw passenger services over the Waterhouses branch withdrawn in September 1935.

Although there were a couple of closures during the 1950s — the Ashbourne branch to passenger services in 1954, the Market Drayton and Leek branches to passengers in 1956, the Trentham branch completely in 1957, the Cold Meece branch in 1958 and the Newfields branch in 1959 — it was to be the 1960s which saw the bulk of the old NSR closed. These closures included the withdrawal of passenger trains over the lines from Burton-on-Trent to Tutbury (June 1960), the Churnet Valley line (November1960), to Cheadle (June 1963), and the Stoke loop (March 1964). The surviving freight sections also rapidly disappeared with the industries that used to support them. These closures included: Grange (October 1961), Audley and Bignall Hill (January 1963), Leek-North Rode (June 1964), Oakamoor-Uttoxeter (January 1965), Market Drayton (May 1967), Congleton-Biddulph (April 1968), Etruria-Hanley (August 1969) and Sandbach (4 January 1971).

Into the 1990s, the surviving sections of the NSR continue to perform a vital role. The line from Macclesfield south through Congleton and Stoke to either Norton Bridge or Colwich is part of the electrified main line between Manchester and London and sees frequent express and local services. The lines from Crewe to Kidsgrove and Stoke to Uttoxeter and on to.Burton on Trent form the core of the Crewe-Derby service. Although freight has diminished significantly with the closure of the local deep mines and the contraction of the pottery industry, there remains considerable freight traffic in the vicinity, although with the closure of Silverdale Colliery the remaining section of the ex-NSR line to Market Drayton (served by the Madeley Chord off the WCML) has been closed. Other surviving stretches of the erstwhile NSR include the closed (but not lifted) branch to Cheadle and the 'mothballed' line from Stoke to the quarry at Caldon Low. The line from Leek Brook Junction to Oakamoor, which was also 'mothballed' is now closed and negotiations are in hand for its sale to the Cheddleton-based North Staffordshire Railway. If successful, the preservationists intend to restore the link from Oakamoor to Alton Towers.

Leek

Then: Undated
The station was situated on the line from Macclesfield Central to Burton on Trent. It opened, along with the line from North Rode to Uttoxeter (the Churnet Valley line) on 13 July 1849.

Now: 7 January 1995
The station remained open until passenger services over the route to Uttoxeter were withdrawn on 4 January 1965; services north to North Rode had been withdrawn on 7 November 1960 and the link to Stoke had been lost on 7 June 1956. Freight facilities continued until July 1970, although the line north to North Rode had been closed completely on 15 June 1964. Today the road bridge remains, but everything else has disappeared. The site, like so many others, has been taken over by a supermarket. I have visited more supermarkets whilst preparing this book than I ever have for shopping!
Ian Allan Library/Author

Rudyard

Then: 9 May 1959
This station was situated just north of Leek on the line to North Rode and, apart from serving the small community of the name, also brought tourists in to the attractive countryside and reservoir. Amongst visitors to the area were Mr and Mrs Kipling, who were so taken with the locality that they named their son, the famous writer, after it. An Ian Allan special, the 'Potteries Express' passes the station headed by 'Crab' 2-6-0 No 42922 of Buxton shed. The special had originated from Paddington.

Now: 7 January 1995
Rudyard lost its passenger services on 7 November 1960 and the railway through the station closed completely four years later. The site of the station is now a car park primarily for walkers and users of the miniature railway, the trackbed of which can be seen on the left of the photograph. The garage-like structure in the background is used as the line's locomotive shed.
H. B. Oliver/Author

Alton

Then: Undated
Situated just south of Oakamoor on the Churnet Valley line, services were inaugurated over the line towards Uttoxeter on 13 July 1849. The ornate style of the building was the result of it being used for the adjacent country house Alton Towers.

Now: 7 January 1995
Passenger services over the line from Leek to Uttoxeter were withdrawn on 4 January 1965 and the section south from Oakamoor was closed completely on 25 January the same year. The section to Oakamoor, now served from Stoke, remained open for freight traffic until 30 August 1988. The line to Oakamoor is now the subject of a preservation project by the Cheddleton-based North Staffordshire Railway. If these plans come to fruition the intention is to extend the line to Alton, thereby adding an additional attraction to the other delights of the Alton Towers theme park. As can be seen the actual station building remains remarkably intact. The view was taken from the road bridge, rather than from platform level, as replicating the original angle would have given a very restricted view. The weather was dismal and the damp mist still lingered among the trees.
Ian Allan Library/Author

Kidsgrove

Then: 13 March 1965
The station illustrated is situated at the junction between the lines from Stoke to Crewe and Manchester. Now called Kidsgrove, the station was originally entitled Harecastle and the first Kidsgrove station was situated on the loop line to Stoke via Tunstall and Burslem. The loop line lost its passenger services on 2 March 1964. Railways first reached the station on 9 October 1848 when the line from Stoke to Crewe was opened throughout and the section from Harecastle to Congleton was also opened. Here Fowler 2-6-4T, on a Manchester University Railway Society special, is seen coming off the lines from Crewe. This locomotive, based at Stockport shed, was typical of those which worked local passenger services in the area for many years.

Now: 7 January 1995
The station has been much rebuilt and the main line towards Manchester electrified. Despite appearances to the contrary, the 25kV does not as yet stretch as far as Crewe. Class 150/1 No 150123 calls to collect a few passengers on the 14.19 Nottingham-Crewe service.
Author (2)

Stoke on Trent

Then: 13 July 1962
Railways came to Stoke on Trent in April 1848 when the line south to Norton Bridge was opened. Stoke was the headquarters of the NSR and a sizeable network of lines developed around it. A Midland Class 4F 0-6-0, a type of locomotive used for many years in the area, heads an up mineral train into the station. Note the pottery kilns, which gave the region its nickname of the Potteries, in the distance.

Now: 7 January 1995
Although the network of lines serving Stoke has been diminished, the impressive station remains. It has been refurbished and the up platform extended. The station is an important intermediate station on the electrified services to the northwest and a DVT at the rear of the 10.50 Euston-Manchester service is seen departing with Class 08 No 08585 parked on the up side.
G. D. King/Author

Stone

Then: Undated
The very fine station at Stone, opened in 1848, is located at the junction of the lines from Stoke to Norton Bridge/Stafford and Colwich Junction. The station became a junction with the opening of the Colwich line on 1 May 1849.
Now: 7 January 1995
Fortunately the attractive building still stands but externally looks run down. The only occupants appeared to be a local taxi office. The platforms for the main line to Colwich have been removed, but those on the Norton Bridge line remain to serve the local EMUs on the service from the north to Stafford and beyond. Class 304 No 304009 is seen in the station with a southbound service.
Ian Allan Library/Author

Birkenhead Joint Railway

The origins of the Birkenhead Joint line date back to the 1830s and the promotion of the Chester & Birkenhead Railway. This railway was authorised by an Act of 1837 and was opened on 23 September 1840. The line was taken over by the Birkenhead, Lancashire & Cheshire Junction Railway in 1847, under whose auspices the line from Chester to Warrington was opened on 18 December 1850.

In August 1859 the line became the Birkenhead Railway and on 20 November 1860 it was taken over jointly by the London & North Western and Great Western railways. It remained a joint line until Nationalisation in 1948. The line from Hooton, on the Birkenhead line, to Helsby, on the line to Warrington, opened on 1 July 1863. This was followed by a line westwards from Hooton to Parkgate, which opened on 1 October 1866. The grand terminus of the line, the much-lamented Birkenhead

(Woodside), opened on 31 March 1878. The line's final extension, from Parkgate to link with the Wirral Railway at West Kirby opened on 19 April 1886.

At the Grouping in 1923 the Birkenhead Joint passed to the LMS and the enlarged GWR and it was not until the post 1948 era that significant changes occurred. The line from Hooton to West Kirby lost its passenger services on 17 September 1956 and was closed completely in May 1962. The station at Birkenhead (Woodside), along with the line from there to Rock Ferry, closed on 5 November 1967 and the station at Woodside has been subsequently demolished. From 1985 electric services, which had operated courtesy of the Mersey Railway to Rock Ferry, were extended to Hooton. Electric services were further extended to Chester and Ellesmere Port in 1993 and 1994 respectively.

Helsby

Then: 17 July 1948
This was the junction where the Birkenhead Joint line from Hooton met the company's route from Chester to Warrington. Although not visible in the photographs, the Cheshire Lines Committee route from Mouldsworth passed over the Chester line before joining the line towards Hooton. The line from Chester to Warrington opened on 18 December 1850, although Helsby did not gain a station until two years later. It became a junction on 1 July 1863 with the opening of the route from Hooton. The Midland Compounds worked the Liverpool and Manchester expresses to North Wales for many years until the early 1950s and No 1150 is shown leaving on the 7.50am from Llandudno to Liverpool
Now: 12 January 1995
Although the ex-CLC Helsby & Alvanley station lost its passenger services in 1964 that line survives as an out of use freight-only route. Both the ex-Birkenhead Joint routes survive. Prior to the electrification of the Merseyrail services to Chester and Ellesmere Port, a DMU service used to link Helsby with Hooton. A Liverpool-Ellesmere Port service operated by Pacers now runs as is shown in this picture of Class 142 No 142035 leaving on the 10.22 departure from Ellesmere Port.
R. Whitfield/Author

Norton (Runcorn East)

Then: 28 October 1956
This station was situated on the Chester-Warrington line between Frodsham and Warrington and was closed on 1 September 1952. More than four years later the station remained intact as this local stopping train, hauled by Class 5 No 45441, was halted here. The original caption records 'The pilot man gives instructions to the driver of the ordinary stopping passenger train to Chester ... whilst the firemar goes to change the headlights'.
Now: 12 January 1995
The new signalbox, constructed since the demolition of the original station, retains the name Norton, although the new station, opened on 3 October 1983, is called Runcorn East. Class 60 No 60084 *Cross Fell* passes the site of the old station heading an empty oil train from Hunslet to Stanlow.
N. Jones/Author

Thurstaston

Then: 30 April 1952

The Birkenhead Joint line from Hooton to West Kirby ran along the west coast of the Wirral peninsula. The line opened from Hooton to Parkgate on 1 October 1866 and thence, via Thurstaston, to West Kirby on 19 April 1886. Reflecting the fact that the Birkenhead Joint was an LMS/GWR line, ex-GWR 0-6-0PT No 3776 awaits the down local to clear the single line section to West Kirby.

Then: 12 January 1995

Passenger services over the Hooton-West Kirby line were withdrawn on 1 February 1954, although freight survived until 1962. A coal depot continued to operate here, albeit not rail-served, until 1976. The area has now been converted into a park and walkway. Although shrouded in new bushes, the platforms still survive.

R. Hewitt/Author

Hooton

Then: 5 March 1967
Crewe North-based Stanier Class 5 No 44680 heads for Chester on a Stephenson Locomotive Society special on the last day of regular steam services to Birkenhead from Chester. The line from Helsby Joins in the distance from the right.
Now: 12 January 1995
The trackworks has been rationalised as can be seen in this photograph of Class 508 EMU No 508103 approaching the station on the 14.19 train from Chester to Liverpool (Central).
Author (2)

Rock Ferry

Then: 27 July 1963
Fowler 2-6-4T No 42247 is shown approaching the station with the 8.55am Birkenhead-Paddington express. The station at Rock Ferry dates from 31 October 1862, when it was opened to replace a station, Rock Lane, which had been opened in 1846. The new station was about 400yd nearer to Birkenhead.
Now: 12 January 1995
The through services from London to Birkenhead ceased on 5 March 1967 when Birkenhead (Woodside) closed. Rock Ferry was the terminus of electric services until the third-rail electrified route was extended to Chester and Ellesmere Port in 1993 and 1994 respectively. Class 508 EMU No 508117 is pictured arriving at the station with a train to Chester. The signalbox, albeit relatively modern, was demolished as part of the electrification project and the consequent resignalling. The little-used line on the right leads to the dock area.
N. Matthews/Author

Mersey Railway

The first proposals for a railway tunnel under the River Mersey were made in the 1860s, when a pneumtically-powered line was promoted. This, however, came to naught and it was to be almost 20 years before the steam-operated Mersey Railway line was officially opened by the Prince of Wales on 20 January 1886.

Public services between Green Lane and St James, Liverpool, were inaugurated on 1 February 1886. The branch to Birkenhead Park opened on 2 January 1888 and the original line was extended to Rock Ferry on 15 June 1891. A further extension saw the line extended to Liverpool Central (Low Level) on 11 January 1892. All was not right with the company, however; steam operation over the steeply graded lines was problematic and the company also faced financial difficulties, being effectively bankrupt in 1892. A new board of directors took over and, following consultation, decided on the electrification of the line. An agreement of 1899 with George Westinghouse, an American who was keen to develop

business for the British arm of his business, led to the electrification of the line. The new electrified services commenced on 3 May 1903, making the Mersey Railway the first in Britain to be converted from steam to electric power.

Following pressure from the company, the Mersey Railway was excluded from the 1923 Grouping and therefore retained its independence right to Nationalisation in 1948. Even before Nationalisation, there had been pressure to construct a line linking all the main line stations in Liverpool, but this was not to come to fruition until the 1970s. The line to Central (Low Level) lost its passenger services on 18 July 1975, although it survives as a link between the Mersey and Wirrral sections of the electrified routes, to facilitate the construction of the single-track loop from St James, via new deep level stations at Central and Lime Street back to St James. The modernised Mersey Railway now forms the core of an electrified network that spreads out into the Wirral peninsula and reaches as far south as Chester.

Birkenhead Central

Then: 1981
The Mersey Railway station at Birkenhead Central dates from the opening of the line in 1886. The Mersey Railway was authorised to electrify its services in 1900 and the new electric trains were brought into operation on 3 May 1903. A Class 503 EMU, No M28381, is pictured ready to depart towards Rock Ferry, where the Mersey Railway shared the station with the Birkenhead Joint. The Class 503s were introduced in 1938 with a further batch built in 1956. No M28381 was one of those from the second batch.
Now: 12 January 1995
Almost 15 years later, little, other than changes in rolling stock and platform signage, seems to have altered. Birkenhead Central remains busy as two Class 508s prepare to depart — No 508127 for Liverpool (Central) and No 508103 for Chester. The depot can be seen on the right of the picture.
J. S. Burnley/Author

Wirral Railway

Although the Wirral Railway inherited by the LMS was a relatively small concern, its history was fairly complex. Its origins dated back to the 1860s when the Hoylake Railway was authorised to construct a line from Hoylake to Seacombe with a branch to Birkenhead Dock. The section from Hoylake to Birkenhead Dock was opened on 2 July 1877; it was extended from Hoylake to West Kirby on 1 April 1878. Whilst it had yet to reach one of its original targets, the company renamed itself the Seacombe, Hoylake & Deeside Railway on 18 June 1881.

Two years later the first Wirral Railway was incorporated with powers to construct a line from the docks to link up with the Mersey Railway at Birkenhead Park; this line opened on 2 January 1888.

Back with the SH&DR, 2 January 1888 also witnessed the opening of that company's branch to Wallasey and, two months later, the branch was extended to its final terminus at New Brighton.

On 11 June 1891 the SH&DR and original Wirral companies were to merge as an enlarged Wirral Railway. It was, ironically, under the auspices of the new company that the line to Seacombe was finally opened on 1 June 1895. Given the contemporary moves towards electrifying the adjacent Mersey Railway, it was not surprising that the Wirral Railway contemplated a similar move as early as 1900, but it was not to be until 14 March 1938, under the aegis of the LMS (which had taken over in 1923), that the lines from Birkenhead to New Brighton and West Kirby were electrified.

A total of 10.5 route miles was electrified from that date and new through services started to run through to Liverpool Central over the metals of the still-independent Mersey Railway. Excluded from the electrification plans was the branch to Seacombe.

Nationalisation brought the Mersey and Wirral railways under single management for the first time. However, the lines of the ex-Wirral Railway were not to survive intact for long; the non-electrified branch to Seacombe lost its passenger services on 4 January 1960 and was closed completely on 17 June 1963.

Electric services have now been operating over the former Wirral Railway routes for almost 60 years; apart from the introduction of replacement rolling stock and the completion of the Liverpool loop line, the lines remain remarkably unchanged.

New Brighton

Then: 27 July 1960
The line to New Brighton was constructed by the Seacombe, Hoylake & Deeside Railway and was opened from Wallasey to New Brighton on 30 March 1888. The bulk of the Wirral Railway was electrified from 14 March 1938 and one of the 19 three-car sets built for the service in 1938, headed by No M28682M, is shown ready to depart from the terminus with a service for Liverpool (Central).
Now: 12 January 1995
Today, 35 years on, little has changed. Electric services, now dominated by the Class 508 units, continue. One of these three-car sets, No 508118, in the attractive yellow livery of Merseyrail, is caught ready to depart with a Liverpool-bound service.
A. H. Bryant/Author

Cumbria

Furness Railway

The Furness Railway was one of the relatively small regional railways that the LMS inherited in 1923. Incorporated on 23 May 1844 it initially constructed a minor network of lines serving Barrow-in-Furness primarily for freight from Crooklands and Kirkby to the docks. Passenger services, which were introduced over the line to Dalton (just west of the terminus at Crooklands), started in August 1846 and passenger trains also operated over the line to Piel Pier in connection with shipping services.

The bulk of what was later to form the FR at Grouping was, however, to be built by a separate company, the Whitehaven & Furness Junction Railway, which the FR took over in 1865. This railway was authorised to build a link between Whitehaven and an extension of the FR's Kirkby line to Foxfield and Broughton. The coastal route from Whitehaven was opened in three stages: to Ravenglass on 21 July 1849; thence to Bootle on 8 July 1850; and finally to Foxfield on 1 November 1850.

The next phase of the FR's development was the construction of the line eastwards from Crooklands to Ulverston. This was opened in two stages: from Crooklands to Lindal on 6 May 1851 and thence to Ulverston on 7 June 1854. Beyond Ulverston the construction of the line to Carnforth was again under the aegis of a separate company — although with close links to the FR — the Ulverstone (sic) & Lancaster Railway. This route was opened on 26 August 1857. The U&LR was taken over by the FR in 1862.

Apart from the main line the FR was also involved with a number of other lines. Of these the most important was the joint line with the Midland that linked Carnforth with the Midland line at Wennington, which opened on 6 June 1867. This line was important for the FR as it allowed the company to play-off the Midland with the LNWR; this was particularly important as the latter company controlled railways at both ends of the FR.

The FR also built two branches to tap into the tourist market of the Lake District. The first was the branch from Foxfield and Broughton to Coniston, which was opened on 18 June 1859. The second, which ultimately served Lake Windermere, was completed in 1869.

The last major section of line to be opened outside Barrow was the link from Arnside northwards to a junction with the LNWR at Hincaster, which was opened on 26 June 1876.

Although the tourist traffic to the Lakes was important the late 19th century saw an economic boom in the region, with the development of iron ore extraction and the dramatic growth of Barrow as an industrial centre. To cater for these trends, the FR undertook dramatic changes to the railways of Barrow itself in the early 1880s. These changes included the completion of the loop line on the west side of the peninsula to form a triangular junction with the original line north to Kirkby. Also completed at this time was the line from St Lukes Junction to Ormsgill Junction, on which was situated Barrow Central station — the FR's most impressive station — which was opened in 1882.

Apart from a minor closures in Barrow, which were partly the result of the 1882 enlargement, the entire FR network passed to the LMS in 1923. During the interwar years there were some relatively minor casualties; for example, the line to Piel Pier lost its passenger services on 6 July 1936. The first major withdrawal of passenger services occurred on 25 September 1938 when passenger services were withdrawn from the branch to Lakeside (summer excursion traffic continued until 6 September 1965) and this was followed on 4 May 1942 when the line between Arnside and Hincaster lost them.

After Nationalisation, the pace of closure accelerated. Passenger services over the Coniston branch were withdrawn on 6 October 1958 with freight services succumbing on 30 April 1962. Final closure of the section from Lakeside to Haverthwaite came on 6 September 1965, although this section has subsequently been preserved. Unfortunately, road construction makes it impossible to regain the junction at Plumpton; the final section of the line, from Plumpton to Backbarrow closed on 24 April 1967. There has also been a rationalisation of the lines in the Barrow region, a reflection of the decline in the region's industrial base.

However, despite the closures, there remains much of the old FR. The main line from Carnforth to Barrow and thence along the coast to Whitehaven remains, as does the former joint line to Wennington junction. Ironically, the latter line has outlived the ex-Midland line it was built to connect with.

Ravenglass

Then: 23 July 1952
The fine FR station stands out well in this picture of an up local freight collecting wagons from the Ravenglass & Eskdale Railway sidings. The locomotive is ex-L&YR 0-6-0 No 52418, which spent its last years of operation allocated to this area. Note the staggered platforms. The 15in narrow gauge line was created by the famous model engineer, W. J. Bassett-Lowke back in 1915, after the original 3ft gauge line had closed in 1913. The signalbox, out of the picture and behind the photographer, was in a well-elevated situation at the top of the embankment, set back from the track. Although disused, the box still exists.
Now: 6 December 1994
The station is still in existence (as a restaurant) and the staggered platforms remain. Sellafield nuclear power station can just be seen on the skyline. The Ravenglass & Eskdale Railway has moved into the goods yard, and the former goods shed is now in use by the narrow gauge line.
A. Newton/Author

Foxfield

Then: September 1954
This delightful station was opened back in August 1858, but enlarged in 1879. Being the junction for the line, it is always, of course associated with the Coniston branch, and the picture shows Fowler 2-6-4T No 42364, which was no doubt allocated to Barrow, about to depart northwards. Originally, on the opening of the Whitehaven & Furness Junction Railway, the junction for the Coniston branch was situated at Broughton in Furness.
Now: 6 December 1994
Apart from the station building over the platform, much still remains. The signalbox is still necessary to control the level crossing at the south end of the station. The water tank is in place as is the wooden shelter on the platform behind the box. At dusk Class 31 No 31233 *Severn Valley Railway* pauses on a nuclear flask train for Sellafield before heading north.
Ian Allan Library/Author

Barrow Central

Then: 1931

An up train prepares to leave with the impressive combination of an ex-LNWR 2-4-0 No 5104 *Woodkirk* piloting one of the very impressive ex-FR Baltic tanks No 11102.

The timber-framed station with its overall roof was opened in 1882, but was eventually destroyed in an air raid in May 1941. Just to the left, but out of the picture, the ex-FR 0-4-0 *Coppernob* used to be kept in a glass pavilion, but this was also destroyed and the locomotive was sent to Horwich Works for safekeeping. The locomotive finally went to the National Railway Museum.

Now: 5 December 1994

The new station was built in 1959 and all passenger traffic is now accommodated by the two platforms illustrated. The station is well-kept, but the volume of traffic, especially heading north, is nothing like what it used to be. Freight traffic has virtually disappeared from the once busy industrial area, except for nuclear flask trains to Sellafield. Class 156 No 156428 has just arrived in torrential rain on the 11.48 from Manchester Airport.

J. Coltas/Author

Ulverston

Then: August 1965
A Morecambe-Lakeside through train is seen waiting to leave after reversing headed by Lancaster-based Ivatt 2-6-0 No 46441. Happily the locomotive is now preserved and is currently active on main line tours. The station was undoubtedly the finest on the Furness Railway comprising an island platform and one platform on the down. By complete chance the tower clock is showing virtually the same time in both photographs.
Now: 5 December 1994
The station is still in an excellent state of repair and must be one of the finest small stations in the country. The paintwork and platform surfaces are not quite as tidy as they were a few years ago, but nevertheless it is a pleasure to visit. Pacer No 142035 has just arrived in the pouring rain working the 13.33 from Barrow to Lancaster. The station was built in 1878 to replace poor facilities and was designed by Lancaster architects, Paley and Austin, who were well known in the area for the design of local churches.
W. H. Foster/Author

Lakeside

Then: 29 May 1960
The 745ft long platform 1 is occupied by a Stephenson Locomotive Society special hauled by Stanier 2-6-0 No 42952 returning tender first to Plumpton Junction. It was obviously a busy Saturday with Fairburn 2-6-4T No 42120 ready to return to Barrow, whilst Aston-allocated Class 5 No 45314 waits to join its train. The steamers on Lake Windermere berth by the end of the coaches on the right-hand side. At this date the location was virtually complete.

Then: 22 August 1964
Four years on from the previous picture, part of the yard had been dismantled, although the camping coach was still *in situ*. One of the 20 Metropolitan-Vickers Class 28 Co-Bo Type 2s, which worked out the latter years of their short careers in the Barrow area, is ready to leave with a special formed of non-corridor stock. The line closed on 6 September 1965, just a year after the date of this picture.

Now: 5 December 1994
Today, for most of the year, tourists to the Lake District can still travel by steam train to Lakeside and transfer to a boat for a trip on Lake Windermere. The long platform is still in use, while the other line is normally used for running round the locomotives. The yard on the left was occupied by magnificent yachts on my visit. The signal gantry is still in use, but with only half the signals.
Author (3)

Haverthwaite

Then: 2 September 1965
This delightful station, situated between two short tunnels, closed to passenger traffic on 30 September 1946. It once had a goods yard, but this has now been converted into a car park for the preserved Lakeside & Haverthwaite Railway. Ivatt 2-6-0 No 46441 passes the yard, which was then in use, heading for Lakeside. This photograph was taken before the line's complete closure by BR.

Now: 5 December 1994
The line remained open for excursion traffic until 6 September 1965. The line towards Plumpton Junction was demolished as part of a road widening scheme, but the section to Lakeside was taken over by the Lakeside & Haverthwaite Railway and reopened on 20 May 1973. The reopening ceremony was performed by the then Bishop of Wakefield, better known to enthusiasts as the photographer Eric Treacy. Today the station is the main operating centre of the railway. The corner of the large shed which houses the rolling stock can just be seen on the left, with the car park directly behind. The line has two ex-BR 2-6-4Ts but is often worked by ex-industrial engines. Shunting of coaches by two ex-BR Class 03 diesels was taking place at the time of my visit.
D. A. Idle/Author

Grange-over-Sands

Then: 10 September 1960
The present attractive station building dates from the 1870s, although the line opened in August 1857. Grange developed after the arrival of the railway into a holiday resort, with a promenade alongside the railway. It is not many years ago since the through services from Barrow to Euston were withdrawn. Fowler '4F' No 44277 is shown leaving with a pick-up freight for Carnforth and beyond.

Now: 5 December 1994
Very little has altered over the 34 years between these pictures except for the new traction and lack of freight in any quantity. Even the weather on the two days appeared to be similar. With a very rough sea pounding the promenade Class 156 No 156440 leaves on the 12.21 from Barrow to Lancaster.
D. Singleton/Author

Arnside

Then: 17 April 1968
Arnside station was part of the Ulverstone & Lancaster Railway which opened in 1857. The route included two long cast-iron viaducts over the rivers Kent and Leven. It was the last section to be built in the link between Cumbria and the main line at Carnforth. The line was taken over by the Furness Railway in 1862. Only a few months before the end of steam on BR one of the surviving Class 5s, No 45391 based at Carnforth, heads west with a brake van.

Now: 5 December 1994
Little seems to have altered during the last 25 years, except the condition of the platforms have deteriorated and the station lights appear to have been renewed. The 10.53 Barrow-Manchester Airport service, comprised of Sprinter No 156428, is shown passing non-stop. *R. Siviter/Author*

Carnforth

Then: 24 May 1968
Locally-based Class 9F 2-10-0 No 92077 is piloted by Type 2 (later Class 25) No D7528 (renumbered under the TOPS scheme 25178) as they haul a heavy oil train from Heysham Moss to Leeds through the FR/MR platforms at the station. The train will head over the ex-Midland Railway metals towards Wennington Junction before heading east into Yorkshire. Carnforth was originally served by LNWR services over the Preston-Carlisle route and by Midland and Furness services.

Now: 27 December 1994
Whilst not visible in the photograph, the platforms on the West Coast main line were taken out of service in 1970 and have been subsequently demolished leaving only the ex-FR/MR platforms to accommodate services. The goods yard on the right-hand side has become the car park for the Steamtown museum complex. Class 47 No 47340, in departmental livery, has just arrived from the Barrow direction.
D. Cross/Author

Maryport & Carlisle Railway

With a route mileage of less than 43 and with a total of only some 30 locomotives being passed to the LMS in 1923, the Maryport & Carlisle was one of the smallest of the pre-Grouping companies and yet, despite its size, it retained its independence (except for a short period when the 'Railway King' George Hudson held sway) from its incorporation in 1837 through to the Grouping. Although small, the railway was highly profitable as it carried considerable mineral traffic to the harbour at Maryport.

The Maryport & Carlisle Railway was authorised by an Act of 12 July 1837, which had been promoted by Humphrey Senhouse, whose family had been influential in the development of Maryport as a major harbour, and had George Stephenson as engineer. The first section, from Arkleby Pits south to Maryport was opened on 15 July 1840. This was extended northwards to Aspatria on 12 April 1841. The next stage to be opened was the connection at Carlisle with the Newcastle & Carlisle Railway southwards to Wigton on 10 May 1843 and thence to Brookfields on 2 December 1844. Also on 2 December 1844 the section from Aspatria to Low Row was opened, leaving the final section of the main line — from Low Row to Brookfields — to open on 10 February 1845. Thus the line from Maryport to Carlisle was opened throughout. Between 1848 and 1850 the line was leased to George Hudson, but his impact was to cause the line financial problems.

Apart from the main line, the M&CR was also involved with two other lines. The route from Aspatria, via Mealsgate, to Leegate opened in 1866 and the Derwent branch, from Bullgill Junction to Papcastle opened in 1867. This latter line, built as a defensive measure against the threat posed by the Cockermouth, Keswick & Penrith Railway and the LNWR saw the M&CR gain runing powers over the LNWR lines in the area and vice versa. It was thus possible to operate a Maryport-Cockermouth service. At Linefoot, on the Derwent branch, there was a line opened in the 1880s by the Whitehave, Cleator & Egremont Railway which provided an alternative route into Workington.

The first section of the M&CR succumbed prior to the 1923 Grouping, when, on 1 August 1921, services were withdrawn from the section north of Mealsgate to Wigton. This section of the line had already been closed once before (shortly after it had opened). All the rest of the M&CR passed to LMS ownership, although the majority of the company's locomotive fleet were quickly withdrawn with the last two succumbing in 1933 and 1934.

By that time the ex-M&CR had shrunk yet further with the withdrawal of the Aspatria-Mealsgate service on 22 September 1930. Freight over this section was to survive until complete closure on 1 December 1952. Shortly after the last Maryport locomotives were withdrawn, services over the Bullgill Junction-Brigham route ceased. This meant that by Nationalisation in 1948 BR inherited the main Maryport-Carlisle route and the freight-only branch to Mealsgate. Of the nine intermediate stations between Maryport and Carlisle, three lost their passenger services on 5 June 1950 (Dearham Bridge, Brayton and Leegate), one on 12 June 1950 (Curthwaite), one on 18 June 1951 (Cummersdale) and one on 7 March 1960 (Bullgill). This leaves three intermediate stations — Aspatria,

Wigton and Dalston — at which the surviving local services call.

Now shorn of its branch lines, but with several freight terminals still extant, the Maryport-Carlisle route remains an important railway artery. Whilst not as profitable as it was in the late 19th century, when the combined coal and haematite reserves made the railways of the district amongst the most financially successful of all the pre-Grouping companies, the line continues to play host to local passenger services between Carlisle and Workington as well as a variety of freight trains.

Workington

Then: 3 May 1958
Carlisle Upperby Class 5 No 45258 is seen ready to leave with a train for the south. Workington was the centre of the railway network in west Cumbria, which served the extensive steel and coal mining industries in the area. The LNWR and FR took over the smaller companies in the mid-1860s. The main depot in the area was at Workington, and in the mid-1950s had an allocation of 28 engines. It eventually closed on 1 January 1968.

Now: 6 December 1994
The condition of the platforms and station roof have deteriorated considerably between the dates of these pictures. The two centre lines now appear to be little used, and what freight that still exists appears to use the line at the back of the half-demolished station wall on the left-hand side. The passenger service between Carlisle and Whitehaven still offers an hourly service, with some trains continuing through to Barrow. Tyne & Wear Pacer in yellow livery No 142056 is shown leaving for Whitehaven on the 10.58 from Carlisle.
J. C. W. Halliday/Author

Maryport

Then: Unknown

Close examination of the numberplate on the side of the locomotive reads 'M&C R1'. This very early picture is of one of the line's 2-4-0s built by the railway around 1876 in Maryport. The Maryport & Carlisle Railway was the oldest company (in terms of unchanged name) to become part of the LMS, having opened in stages between 1840 and 1845, and was always a profitable operation. The train is shown against the impressive station building which also served as the company's offices.

Now: 6 December 1994

The single platform arrangement at the station has continued after the fine buildings were demolished in 1960. Today only the glorified bus shelter remains, and the extensive shunting yards are either out of use or been lifted, although there are still through running lines avoiding the platform. The line still enjoys an hourly service to both Carlisle and Whitehaven operated by Pacers and Sprinters.

Ian Allan Library/Author

Whitehaven, Cleator & Egremont Railway

The WC&ER was promoted as a line that would facilitate the opening up of the West Cumberland iron ore fields and, indeed, during the late 19th century the region was to benefit considerably from the exploitation of the region's mineral resources.

The railway was incorporated on 16 June 1854 to construct a line inland from Mirehouse Junction (near Whitehaven) to Moor Row and thence to Egremont with a short branch from Moor Row to Frizington. It opened for mineral services on 11 January 1856 and to passengers 18 months later, on 1 July 1857. An extension from Frizington into Eskett and Rowrah was authorised and mineral services started over this line in November 1862. Passenger services were extended to Rowrah in February 1864. The next phase saw the line extended further north from Rowrah to a junction at Marron with the Whitehaven-Cockermouth line; mineral services over this route were introduced on 15 January 1866 with passenger trains on 2 April the same year.

The year 1866 also saw the opening, at Moor Row, of the first of the company's deviation lines, which were built to obviate problems caused by subsidence — the result of ore extraction along the route of the line.

The company's final extension, from Egremont to join the Furness Railway at Sellafield opened on 2 August 1869. The FR played an important role with the WC&ER; indeed, half the company's shares were in fact held by its larger neighbour. The remainder were held by the LNWR.

By the date of the Grouping the great days of the West Cumberland iron industry were already past and the inevitable process of rationalisation set in. Passenger services over the Moor Row-Marron section were withdrawn on 13 April 1931 and the final passenger services over the ex-WC&ER, from Whitehaven to Egremont and Sellafield succumbed on 7 January 1935.

Although passenger services had ceased before Nationalisation, BR inherited the entire WC&ER network over which freight trains were still operating. The first casualty occurred on 3 May 1954 when the section from Rowrah to Marron was closed completely. However, the rest of the railway was to survive virtually intact until 19 January 1970 when the section from Beckermet to Sellafield was closed completely. This was followed in 1978 by the closure of British Steel's quarry at Rowrah which led to the lifting of the line from Moor Row to Rowrah two years later.

The final nail in the WC&ER's coffin came with the closure of the last working haematite mine at Beckermet in October 1980. This meant that all traffic over the line from Whitehaven to Beckermet via Moor Row ceased. The section beyond Moor Row has been lifted but the line to Moor Row survives, at the time of writing, in a disused state.

Moor Row

Then: 3 August 1953
The station had closed to regular passenger traffic 18 years before this picture was taken, but it remained open for workmen's trains and special excursions. The only ex-LMS '4F' to be allocated to Moor Row (12E) in 1953, No 44461, prepares to leave on a Bank Holiday special to Morecambe. Moor Row was the centre of the iron mining industry in the area, and had a depot which was situated behind the photographer about 300yd down the line; it closed on 31 July 1954.
Now: 6 December 1994
A local resident walks his dog along the footpath where once the track was laid through the station. Little remains in the area today to indicate what a hive of activity it used to be before the early 1950s. The coast to coast walk from St Bees to Robin's Hood Bay passes this site.
W. A. Camwell/Author

Cleator & Workington Junction

Distington Junction

Then: September 1954

This was the junction where the former Cleator & Workington Junction Railway was joined by the Whitehaven, Cleator & Egremont Railway, which had come up from the coast at Parton. The station appears to have been out of use for some time and the freight traffic appears to be very light. Details of the special are not recorded. The ex-C&WR lines to Cleator and Moor Row closed to all traffic 1 July 1963 and the ex-WC&ER section from Distington to Harrington on 15 June 1964.

Now: 6 December 1994

This particular comparison caused considerable difficulties; there is nothing to suggest a railway existed at this site except the embankment in the foreground which was where the line crossed the road on a bridge. I am only 99% certain that I have found the correct site.

Ian Allan Library/Author

Cockermouth, Keswick & Penrith Railway

Although a line traversing the northern part of the Lake District was promoted in the 1840s, it was not until the 1860s, and the construction of the line over Stainmore that these proposals became a reality.

The Cockermouth, Keswick & Penrith Railway was incorporated in 1861 and was opened for mineral traffic in October 1864. Following an act of 1863 all traffic, with the exception of mineral traffic (which was initially very heavy), was worked by the London & North Western Railway; mineral traffic was worked by the North Eastern Railway. The importance of the line to the LNWR increased with the acquisition by the Euston company of two older railways — the Cockermouth & Workington and the Whitehaven Junction — in 1866. It was via the CK&PR that the LNWR gained access to these remote parts of its empire.

The Whitehaven Junction dated from the late 1840s and represented part of the coastal route from Whitehaven to Maryport. The Cockermouth & Workington was opened in April 1847. Once the LNWR acquired these lines, the basic passenger service over the CK&PR — from Penrith to Workington via Keswick and Cockermouth — was established. This was to survive for a century.

At the eastern end of the CK&PR the NER opened a spur in 1866 southwards to improve access to the Stainmore route, but this declined in importance as the mineral traffic gradually fell away. The link was last used in 1926, but was not officially closed until 1938.

Steam reigned supreme over the line until the arrival of the DMUs in 1955. However, despite the introduction of the new rolling stock, the line could not defy the economics of the early 1960s. Through freight workings were withdrawn on 1 June 1964 and passenger services from Keswick to Workington ceased on 18 April 1966. This meant the total closure of the line west of Keswick. Although facilities were reduced further after 1966, the line was to see final closure to passenger services on 6 March 1972. Freight was to remain operational as far as a quarry west of Blencow until June the same year.

Keswick

Then: 24 August 1963
The station buildings, in the background, used to house the head offices of the Cockermouth, Keswick & Penrith Railway. The impressive Keswick Hotel to the left of the picture was linked directly to the platform via a covered passage, which still exists. Ivatt 2-6-0 No 46432 is shown ready to leave for Penrith on the 8.20am Workington-Manchester Victoria service.
Now: 6 December 1994
The area around the station platform remained derelict for several years after closure on 6 March 1972, although goods workings had ceased from 1 June 1964. The area has now been landscaped and trees planted and, as can be seen, the station still remains intact on the 'down' side. The service to Penrith, during the last years, was a DMU 'shuttle'.
W. G. Sumner/Author

Cockermouth

Then: Undated
The date of this photograph is not recorded, but it was taken after the laying of flat bottomed track. The town first became connected to the railway system as far back as 1847, with the 8½-mile section to Derwent Junction. The station shown was part of the CK&P and dates from 1864. The closure date was April 1966 as with Bassenthwaite Lake, and the buildings remained until they were demolished in 1970. The site apparently then remained unused until 1987. Note the fine gas lamps on the platform.

Now: 6 December 1994
There is virtually nothing left today to indicate that a railway once existed. In fact, I had to seek the assistance of a member of the fire station staff who knew exactly where I should stand in the car park to reproduce the 'Then' picture. The fire station was opened on 30 March 1987 by Cumbria Fire Service and now serves as the brigade's headquarters.
Cecil J. Allen/Author

Bassenthwaite Lake

Then: May 1956
The Cockermouth, Keswick &
Penrith line opened for freight in
November 1864 and to passengers
in January 1865. Bassenthwaite
Lake station was on the section of
line west of Keswick which closed
in April 1966. Ten years before
closure a local freight from
Penrith passes the station as the
signalman holds the tablet for the
next section. The locomotive is
Ivatt 2-6-0 No 46491 which spent
many years working this line. In
1964 the 'Lakes Express', giving
through coaches to Euston, was
still using the line. Even the early
arrival of DMUs to the area was
not enough to save the line.
Now: 6 December 1994
The station can still just be seen
through the trees at the side of the
A66 road. Motorists driving along
the realigned road today will be
unaware that part of the new road
is on the trackbed of this once
attractive section of line.
G. F. Bannister/Author